南京大屠殺
七十年的憶記

THE NANKING MASSACRE
70 YEARS OF AMNESIA

ISBN 978-0-9739183-1-1
PRICE $50

TORONTO ALPHA
78 ST. PATRICK STREET #134
TORONTO, ONTARIO, CANADA M5T 3K8
WWW.TORONTOALPHA.ORG

GRATEFUL ACKNOWLEDGEMENT IS MADE TO THOSE WHO GAVE PERMISSION TO
REPRINT PREVIOUSLY PUBLISHED MATERIALS.

南京大屠殺
七十年的憶記

THE NANKING MASSACRE
70 YEARS OF AMNESIA

DR. JOSEPH Y.K. WONG C.M., IRIS CHANG, AND JOHN FRASER

A Message from John Fraser
Master of Massey College
University of Toronto

Peking Correspondent
1977-1979
The Globe & Mail

Forgetfulness is the balm of victims and the sin of perpetrators. After the end of the Second World War, some Holocaust survivors were only able to rebuild their shattered lives by wiping out virtually all memory of the Nazi concentration camps. In a sinister obverse of this studied and protective amnesia, the perpetrators who committed these vast and grotesque crimes against humanity also forgot everything. This was not merely out of convenience. In time, even camp commandants only seemed to remember the small acts of kindnesses they perpetrated and the excellent sanitary conditions "prevailing" in their "sector."

 In a similar way, time heals many wounds, but time also covers up grievous wrongs. That's why Iris Chang's devastating account of the rape of Nanjing by the occupying Japanese forces is so important: it provides the antidote to criminal amnesia and festering wounds. There is a kind of implicit double standard in the West about the events surrounding the massacres in Nanjing. I suppose some of it is systemic racism: who cares about yellow people killing yellow people. We know now, however, that genocidal slaughter is not restricted to any one creed, colour or ideology (German fascism, Rwandan tribalism, Japanese imperialism). The reality is that the world did not come to fully understand what was in store for it from war-like Japan until Pearl Harbour, despite all the implicit reality of the horrors visited on the citizens of Nanjing in the late nineteen-thirties.

Iris Chang performed a major international public service by passionately reminding an older generation and informing new ones of what happened in Nanjing. It was not just the terror she described, because there were also both implicit and explicit criticisms of Japan for not properly coming to terms with this gruesome heritage. Japan still hasn't and until it learns the lessons Germany has learned in seeking some sort of redemption from past evils through reconciliation and compensation, Nanjing will remain a festering sore. China is no longer mired in static Maoist indolence; it is a giant awakening to the enormous potential of his great people. Japan would be wise to consider 21st-century acts of atonement sooner rather than later. ♠

從60周年到70周年

From the 60th Anniversary to the 70th Anniversary

過去十年來, 加拿大史維會分別在加拿大東西兩岸致力推動亞洲二戰史實的教育和推廣工作。亦是十年前, 即南京大屠殺60周年的日子, 張純如的著作《南京暴行——被遺忘的二戰浩劫》給史維會艱巨的使命帶來了新的希望。猶記當年她出席加拿大史維會為她在溫哥華及多倫多舉行的新書發佈會中, 向熱情期待的讀者介紹自己寫作之心路歷程, 並即場誦讀書中片段。由她還原的一場人類災難, 震撼在場每個人的心靈, 燃起人們追求正義和平的理想。她的著作在過去十年像滾雪球似的啟動了西方世界一場重新認識和保留南京大屠殺史實的運動。她對尋求歷史真相和追求公義的精神和執着亦同時成為我們的激勵。

經過多年的努力和斡旋, 加拿大史維會分別成功取得卑詩省教育廳和安省教育廳的認可, 讓亞洲二戰史實成為高中歷史科的教學參考。純如的著作亦成為後來卑詩省教育廳及卑詩省史維會於2001年合作出版有關亞洲二戰人權教材及多倫多史維會於2005年出版的安省教材時的主要參考書。前者是全球第

In the past 10 years, Canada Association for Learning and Preserving the History of WWII in Asia (ALPHA) has been working hard to promote education and awareness of the World War II history in Asia in both provinces of BC and Ontario in Canada.

It was also 10 years ago, the year of the 60th anniversary of the Nanking Massacre, the book titled "The Rape of Nanking — the Forgotten Holocaust of World War II" written by Iris Chang, brought new hopes to ALPHA.

Being the first book written in English on the subject, with extensive research materials and lots of historical details about the Nanking Massacre, Iris' book shocked the West's conscience and had generated a ripple effect in arousing the interest and awareness of this vastly unknown and one of the darkest chapters of human history.

The memories were so vivid that it seemed like yesterday when Iris presented her book and shared her feelings about her writing process at the book launching events in Vancouver and Toronto. Her courage to seek the truth and her conviction for justice touched and inspired every one of us. We had a strong feeling: how can the world, particularly 1.4 billion Chinese people, put all the burden on her shoulders to unearth and tell the story of the Massacre on our behalf? Iris' book and her spirit brought us not only hope, but also confidence and encouragement that one day the truth about Nanking would be known the world over.

Inspired by Iris, and through many years of hard work and persistence, Canada ALPHA succeeded in gaining the recognition of the Ministries of Education of British Columbia and Ontario to incorporate the Asian holocaust as part of the high school curriculum.

一份以亞洲二戰浩劫為題材教育高中學生世界公民的社會責任的教材。

自2004年起的每年暑期，加拿大史維會組織和資助的「和平與和解──亞洲二戰浩劫史實訪華學習團」已有近百名卑詩省和安省的教育工作者參加。張純如的《南京暴行──被遺忘的二戰浩劫》是行前學習研討會的必讀之書，讓參予老師與當地歷史學家交流和訪問日軍暴行倖存者時，能更深入理解此段史實和背後的歷史教訓。回加後，老師們均積極地將見證帶回社區和校園，和協助推廣這段鮮為人知的人類黑暗史實。明年的學習團，我們希望能邀請其他省份的教育工作者參予，目的是讓這段史實被接受成為全加拿大，甚至世界各地的人道及公義教育之課題。

除了推動亞洲二戰史實在中學的教育，加拿大史維會也透過主辦學術會議，進一步推廣加國人民對此段歷史的認識。2003年在卑詩大學舉行的「防止違反人道罪行──吸取亞洲太平洋戰爭之歷史教訓」學術會議，就是由加拿大史維會聯同日裔加拿大人協會人權委員會，加拿大亞太資源網絡，及三個卑詩大學部門所主辦。張純如應我會之邀擔任主講人，以「種族主義與南京大屠殺」為題，作出透徹的討論和分析，讓其他族裔對亞洲二戰暴行的歷史教訓有深刻的了解。

Iris Chang's book also became a major reference to the teachers' guide on "Human Rights in the Asia Pacific 1931–1945: Social responsibility and Global Citizenship", jointly published by the BC Ministry of Education and BC ALPHA in 2001[1] and the Ontario teaching resource guide published by Toronto ALPHA in 2005.[2] The former is first of its kind in the world featuring human rights violations during WW II in Asia for high school students.

There are close to 100 educators from BC and Ontario who participated in the "Peace and Reconciliation Study Tour" organized and financed by Canada ALPHA since 2004. Iris' book — "The Rape of Nanking" is a must read for their pre-tour preparation to facilitate their better understanding of and deeper reflection on lessons learned from this chapter of history. After returning to Canada, these teachers share their knowledge and testimonies with their colleagues and students. Many of them initiated projects and ideas, with or without support from ALPHA, keeping the promises to the victims, bringing their stories and pain to other parts of the world.

For 2008 Study Tour, we hope to include teachers and educators from other provinces, in addition to Ontario and B.C. We also plan to include Seoul, Korea as the city for in-depth study of the "Comfort Women" system. Our educational initiative has inspired our counterpart in the U.S. to start their own study tours for teachers in 2007.

Apart from promoting Asian holocaust education in school system, Canada ALPHA also holds academic seminars and conferences to raise the awareness of Canadians about the forgotten Asian holocaust. One that was held in 2003 at UBC, titled "Preventing Crimes Against Humanity: Lessons from the Asia Pacific War (1931-1945)"[3] was jointly organized by Canada ALPHA, Human Rights Committee of Japanese Canadian Citizens' Association, Canadian Asian Pacific Resource Network, and three departments of UBC. As our keynote speaker, Iris made a presentation on "Racism and the Rape of Nanking". Her vivid discussion and in-depth analysis allowed the participants of different ethnic backgrounds to have a better understanding of the lessons learnt from this dark chapter of history.

轉眼間, 南京大屠殺70周年的日子將至, 張純如的著作和各地史維會的工作起了非常重要的互動作用。今天的國際輿論對「南京大屠殺」和「從軍慰安婦」等發生在亞洲的二戰暴行已不再完全陌生, 對日本右翼否認史實和推卸罪責的行為不再姑息容忍, 對倖存者的呼求亦不再置若罔聞。

2007年是加拿大史維會一個重要的里程碑。我們感到張純如的精神從未離開。她必定對美國國會通過敦促日本向日軍性奴隸制度的受害婦女道歉的議案感到鼓舞; 對加拿大及世界各地同時推動的類似議案感到欣慰; 亦會為加拿大史維會推動和資助製作的電影「張純如 — 南京大屠殺」中展現她純真而燦爛的笑容。

我們深信這齣以她為主題的電影, 將會感動更多的人。到下一個十年來臨時, 世界將有更多人學會以史為鑑, 反對戰爭, 反對暴力, 堅守公義, 維護和平。

The 70th Anniversary of the Nanking Massacre is fast approaching. The writing of Iris Chang and the efforts of Canada ALPHA and its sister organizations all over the world have contributed to the redress movement of the Asian holocaust victims. Nowadays, Nanking Massacre and Japan's military sexual slavery system (the so-called "Comfort Women") are no longer totally ignored by the international media. The denial of historical facts and the evasion of war crime responsibility by the Japanese right-wingers will no longer be tolerated. The world will no longer be able to disregard the cry for justice from these survivors.

2007 is an important milestone for Canada ALPHA. The unanimous passage of Resolution 121 in the American Congress, urging Japan to 'acknowledge the facts and accept responsibility of the sex slavery system and apologize formally in a clear and unequivocal manner', is a tremendous break-through the world has been waiting for since the end of the war over 60 years ago. Another highly successful 2007 Study Tour, raising the awareness of the public and signing over 40,000 people for its petition to pass a similar motion in the Canadian House of Commons, were all important and significant events to fulfill our mission. The completion of the docudrama 'Iris Chang', of course, caps the very successful year with a big bang. The two stories of the film, one of Iris Chang's courage and conviction to unveil the historical truth, and the other of telling the Nanking atrocity, interweave together so well that we believe it will have a big impact in provoking public awareness of the Nanking Massacre worldwide. It is our fervent hope that the film will be watched by hundreds of millions of people the world over. The legacy of Iris will live forever.

王裕佳, 列國遠

Joseph Wong and Thekla Lit

[1] Ministry of Education, Curriculum Branch, Province of British Columbia (2001), Human Rights in the Asia Pacific 1931–1945: Social responsibility and Global Citizenship — A Resource Guide for Teachers to Support Aspects of Senior Social Studies Curriculum. Co-published by B.C. Association for Learning & Preserving the History of WWII in Asia. [2] Toronto Association for Learning & Preserving the History of WWII in Asia (2005), The Search for Global Citizenship: The Violation of Human Rights in Asia 1931–1945 — A Resource Guide For Ontario Teachers In Canadian And World Studies, Grade 10–12. With the endorsement of Ontario History, Humanities and Social Sciences Teachers' Association and Ontario History, Humanities and Social Sciences Consultants' Association. [3] A Canadian Conference on Global Citizenship — Preventing Crimes Against Humanity: Lessons from the Asia Pacific War (1931–1945). Jointly organized by Canada Association for Learning and Preserving the History of WW II in Asia (ALPHA), Greater Vancouver Japanese Canadian Citizens' Association (JCCA), Canada Asia Pacific Resource Network (CAPRN) and UBC's First Nations House of Learning, International House and Women's Studies and Gender Relations program.

霍可汗，柬埔寨畫家
Lieng Hok, Cambodian artist

甚麼？

What?

南京大屠殺……一個被遺忘了的大浩劫。

Nanking Massacre. The forgotten holocaust.

在那裡？

Where？

Nanking, China.

中國，南京。

誰做的？

Who did it?

為甚麼？

Why?

無言。六星期內屠殺了三十萬條無辜的生命。

Wordless. 300,000 died in six weeks.

甚麼時候？

一九三七年 十二月 十三日。

When?

December 13, 1937.

CORPSES OF NANKING CITIZENS WERE DRAGGED
TO THE BANKS AND THROWN INTO THE RIVER
(MORIYASA MURASE).

Text HUMAN RIGHTS IN THE ASIA PACIFIC
1931–1945: SOCIAL RESPONSIBILITY AND GLOBAL
CITIZENSHIP — A RESOURCE GUIDE FOR TEACHERS
TO SUPPORT ASPECTS OF SENIOR SOCIAL STUDIES
CURRICULUM, MINISTRY OF EDUCATION, PROVINCE OF
BRITISH COLUMBIA, 2001 *Images* REVOLUTIONARY
DOCUMENTS/TAIPEI, PI/BETTMANN

Nanking Massacre

In 1928, the Chinese government moved the capital of China to Nanking. The city normally held about 250,000 people, but by the mid-1930s its population had swollen to more than one million. Many of them were refugees, fleeing from the Japanese armies that had invaded China in 1931.

On November 11, after securing control of Shanghai, the Japanese army advanced towards Nanking. In December 1937, Japanese troops invaded the city of Nanking. Much of the city was destroyed by bombing raids. The Japanese Imperial forces marched thousands of Chinese civilians into the countryside and murdered them; they raped women, and looted and burned people's homes. The large-scale massacre and gross mistreatment of Chinese people at Nanking became

[LEFT] IN NANKING, THE JAPANESE TURNED MURDER TURNED INTO SPORT. NOTE THE SMILES ON THE JAPANESE IN THE BACKGROUND.
[RIGHT] FIVE CHINESE PRISONERS BEING BURIED ALIVE BY THEIR JAPANESE CAPTORS OUTSIDE NANKING AFTER THE FALL OF THE CHINESE CAPITAL.
THIS IS ANOTHER PICTURE SENT TO LOOK MAGAZINE BY W.A. FARMER AFTER IT WAS TAKEN BY A JAPANESE SOLDIER AND SMUGGLED OUT BY
CHINESE FILM SHOP EMPLOYEES WHO "DID THE NATURAL THING IN EXCEEDING THE PRINTING ORDER".

PHOTO BY REVOLUTIONARY DOCUMENTS/TAIPEI

PHOTO BY UPI/BETTMANN

[LEFT] JAPANESE GENERAL MATSUI IWANE RIDES INTO NANKING.
[CENTER] DEAD BODIES OF THE VICTIMS.
[RIGHT] DEAD BODIES LYING IN A DITCH.

known as the Rape of Nanking. The following timeline highlights events related to the massacre.

12 Nov 1937 — Japanese troops capture Shanghai after three months of fierce fighting. The march towards Nanking (now Nanjing) begins and the "Three-all" policy ("Loot all, kill all, burn all") is used to terrorize civilians along the advancing route.

22 Nov 1937 — The International Committee for the Nanking Safety Zone is organized by a group of foreigners to shelter Chinese refugees.

12 Dec 1937 — Chinese soldiers are ordered to withdraw from Nanking.

13 Dec 1937 — Japanese troops capture Nanking.

14 Dec 1937 — The International Committee for the Nanking Safety Zone lodges the first protest letter against the Japanese atrocities with the Japanese Embassy.

19 Feb 1938 — The last of the 69 protest letters against Japanese atrocities is sent by the Safety Zone Committee to the Japanese Embassy and the Committee is renamed as the Nanking International Relief Committee. Many eyewitness accounts of the Nanking Massacre were provided by Chinese civilian survivors and western nationals living in Nanking at the time. The number of Chinese killed in the massacre has been subject to much debate. The Encyclopedia Britannica (1999-2000 Britannica.com) states that estimates of the number of Chinese killed ranges from 100,000 to more than 300,000. The judges for the International Tribunal for the Far East concluded that at least 260,000 people were killed by the Japanese Imperial Army during that period of time.

Several accounts of the Nanking Massacre come from the group of 25 foreigners (mostly American, but also some German, Danish, and Russian people) who had established a neutral area called the International Safety Zone to shelter the Chinese refugees whose lives had been threatened and homes destroyed by the invading Japanese soldiers. When Nanking fell, the Zone housed over 250,000 refugees. The committee members of the Zone found ways to provide these refugees with the basic needs of food, shelter, and medical care. ♦

NOVEMBER, 1937

Shanghai fell to the Japanese Army after 3 months of fierce fighting and heavy casualty on both sides.

JULY 7, 1937

Marco Polo Bridge (Lugou Bridge) Incident marked the beginning of full-scale invasion of China and other Asian countries by Japan.

DECEMBER 13, 1937

Japanese army entered Nanking, the then capital city of China, after days of heavy aerial bombings and surrender of the Chinese troops. A few days before the Japanese took over Nanking, Emperor Hirohito sent his own uncle, Prince Asaka Yasuhiko, to be in charge of the invading troops in Nanking.

NOVEMBER, 1937

Establishment of the International Safety Zone in Nanking by 15 to 20 Westerners, headed by John Rabe, gave refuge to about 250,000 Chinese.

DECEMBER 13, 1937 – EARLY FEBRUARY 1938

Eight weeks of horror — massive killing and raping, resulting in the death of around 300,000 civilians and surrendered Chinese soldiers, and raping of 20,000 to 80,000 women and girls.

DECEMBER 7, 1941

Surprise attack at Pearl Harbour, Hawaii, and subsequently massive assault on the Philippines, Hong Kong, Malaya and Singapore. Hundreds of Canadian soldiers died defending Hong Kong, and close to 1700 were captured.

1940 – 41

The Imperial Japanese forces started the Pacific Offensive, invading Indochina.

AUGUST 6, 1945

The world's first
atomic bomb fell on
Hiroshima.

AUGUST 9, 1945

The second atomic
bomb dropped in
Nagasaki.

1945, SUMMER

Soviet Union entered
the war against Japan.

1937–45

Armed resistance
against Japan con-
tinued throughout
occupied areas in
China and South-
east Asia.

1946–48

The International
Military Tribunal for
the Far East held in
Tokyo. The Japanese
Emperor Hirohito and
all members of the
imperial family were
not prosecuted for
any involvement in
any of the crimes. Up
to 50 suspects were
incarcerated but
released without ever
being brought to trial,
including Nobusuke
Kishi, who later
became the Prime
Minister of Japan.
Many of their descen-
dants have been
holding key positions
in politics and large
corporations.

AUGUST 15, 1945

Japan officially surren-
dered unconditionally,
ending WWII.

1937–97

**The world has
forgotten about
The Rape
of Nanking.**

1951

The San Francisco
Peace Treaty was
signed by 48 allied
countries headed by
U.S. with Japan. Soviet
Union refused to take
part. And the major
victim countries,
China and Korea, were
not invited to join.
The SFPT absolved
Japan of major war
reparations.

NOVEMBER, 1997

Iris Chang's 'The Rape of Nanking — The Forgotten Holocaust of WWII' was published on the 60th Anniversary of the event. It was the first English narrative about the little known horrific chapter of history. This was the first major milestone in the unearthing of the history of the Massacre.

JANUARY, 1997

Toronto ALPHA and B.C. ALPHA worked together to form Canada ALPHA. Calgary and Ottawa ALPHA joined later in the year.

DECEMBER, 1994

Global Alliance for the Preservation of the History of WWII in Asia was formed in San Francisco.

2001

B.C. ALPHA, in association with the Ministry of Education, published the world's first English resource guide on the subject: Human Rights in the Asia Pacific 1931–1945: Social Responsibility and Global Citizenship.

DECEMBER, 1997

The world's first major promotion of Iris Chang's book in Canada, first in Vancouver, then in Toronto, marked the beginning of a new era in the awareness of the history of the Rape of Nanking in the western world. On December 13, 1997, Iris spoke at the Commemorative Concert in Toronto on the Massacre's 60th Anniversary.

2005

The combined lobbying effort of Toronto ALPHA with Ontario educators and teachers resulted in the incorporation of WWII history in Asia in grade 10 History and

Social Studies, both compulsory subjects in Ontario's high schools. The province became the first western jurisdiction to include Asian WWII history in their high school subjects.

Working with teachers and educators in Ontario, Toronto ALPHA published another teaching resource guide, adding the section on grade 10, to B.C. ALPHA's guide.

2004–07

Close to 100 teachers and educators, most of them from B.C. and Ontario, and some from the States have joined our annual study tours to China.

2004

B.C. ALPHA initiated the first Peace and Reconciliation Study Tour to China, for teachers both in B.C. and Ontario. This marked the beginning of our major educational work in Canada on the history of WWII in Asia.

FEBRUARY, 2006

Close to 900 packa of reference book: teaching guides a audio-visual teach aids were delivere to all Ontario high schools, including public, catholic an private high schoc

JUNE 2007 –
AUGUST 2007

40,000 Signatures have been collected in support of the Motion.

MARCH 2007

Media release of the film production in Nanjing, Hong Kong and Seoul.

DECEMBER 13, 2007

70th anniversary date of the beginning of the Nanking Massacre. A commemorative concert will be held in Toronto…

MAY, 2007

Community coalition comprising Chinese, Korean, Filipino and Indonesian communities was formed and has been the driving force for the passing of Motion 291.

OCTOBER 2005 – 07

Idea to produce docudrama of 'Iris Chang' concieved until the completion of the film.

JULY, 2007

The passage of Resolution 121 In the American Congress calling on Japan to formally acknowledge, apologize and accept responsibility in the military sex slavery system known as comfort women marked another significant milestone in the reconciliation and healing process.

NOVEMBER 12, 2007

World premiere of 'Iris Chang, the Rape of Nanking'. The docudrama sets another milestone in provoking worldwide awareness of the Nanking Massacre, and the continued denial and distortion of history by Japan.

MARCH, 2007

Motion 291 which calls for Japanese government's official apology and compensation to the victims of "Comfort Women" was tabled in the House of Commons in Canada.

NOVEMBER ,2007

"Comfort Women" survivors from different countries will be invited to Canada to give testimonies to the Canadian public and Parliament.

JUNE, 2006

Funding for the docudrama 'Iris Chang' secured and production confirmed.

Alison Lee, 13
JAPAN SHOULD APOLOGIZE TO ALL OF THE VICTIMS OF THE FORGOTTEN
HOLOCAUST — THE NANKING MASSACRE. LEARNING AND UNDERSTANDING
THIS TRAGEDY WILL PREVENT HISTORY FROM REPEATING ITSELF.

People Who
Gave Us Hope

John Rabe (1882–1949)

Mr. Rabe, a German businessman working for Siemens in Nanking, China, founded the International Committee in late November 1937, when the Imperial Japanese Army was about to attack Nanjing. The Committee, under his leadership, set up the Nanjing Safety Zone to provide Chinese refugees with food and shelter. He also opened up his own properties to house 650 more refugees. During the massacre, Mr. Rabe and his associates, risking their own lives, tried frantically to stop the rampant atrocities. His courageous efforts helped rescue over 250,000 Chinese from slaughter.

This "Mr. Oskar Schindler of China", also a Nazi, but a kind-hearted one, returned to Germany in 1938, and started a one-man crusade to educate fellow Germans about the Japanese atrocities in Nanjing. The Nazi government quickly arrested him, and confiscated his films but not his paper evidence. Mr. Rabe's 2,000-page diaries are invaluable information on Japanese atrocities.

John Rabe lived in poverty in his last three years of life, and was supported by the food and money sent to him every month by the residents of Nanking in appreciation of his heroic acts. He died of a stroke on January 5, 1949.

Wilhelmina (Minnie) Vautrin (1887 – 1941)

Minnie Vautrin, a Midwest farm girl called to missionary service, devoted her adult life to the education of Chinese women at Ginling Girls College in Nanjing and to helping the poor. In the cauldron of horror that Nanjing became in December 1937, she turned the College into a sanctuary for 10,000 women and girls, and also worked tirelessly with John Rabe in the Nanking Safety Zone. The only weapons this "Goddess of Mercy" had to repel incursions into her college and to protect the refugees in the Nanking Safety Zone were an American flag, and her prayers, wits and immense courage and moral strength.

Weary, stressed and depressed, Miss Vautrin returned to the USA in 1940. She ended her own life a few months later. After the war, the Chinese government awarded her posthumously "The Emblem of the Blue Jade", the highest national honor possible.

Her bronze statue is proudly standing in the campus of Nanjing Normal University, the former site of the Ginling Girls College.

Her diaries, like John Rabe's, are a gold mine of information on Japanese atrocities witnessed in Nanjing.

John Gillespie Magee

Rev. Magee was an American missionary working in Nanking at the time of the Massacre. He was also one of the members of the International Committee on Nanking Safety Zone. Rev. Magee had taken film footage of a lot of atrocities carried out by the Japanese Imperial Army in Nanking. The footage about the Massacre was smuggled out the occupied territories at great risk to lives. They later became key evidence at the International War Crimes Tribunal for the Far East, exposing the truth of the extent of the rape and murder in Nanking during that period. The visual documentation, together with diaries of other Westerners like John Rabe and Minnie Vautrin, are invaluable archives for subsequent historians and film-makers to reconstruct the horrors of the Rape in Nanking in the winter of 1937–1938. The evidence presented by these footages proves to be too powerful for denial by Japanese history revisionists.

Professor Saburo Ienega

For 35 years, this distinguished historian and educator challenged the Japanese government in court on their censorship of history textbooks authored by him. Professor Ienaga has dedicated his life to the mission that Japanese young people are able to learn the truth about their own country's recent history and to learn lessons of humanity from it.

More than 10,000 support letters were collected across Canada and sent to the Japanese government in support of Ienaga in 1997 which helped win the ruling by the Japanese supreme court that the censoring of the facts of Unit 731 in the history textbook of Professor Ienega by the Japanese Ministry of Education was illegal.

Professor Ienega was nominated Nobel Peace Price for the year 2001. 251 distinguished professors of history, law, philosophy and political science, and also 19 parliamentarians from different countries nominated Prof Ienaga.

Iris Chang (1968 – 2004)

This award-winning Chinese American author is best remembered for her meticulously researched, powerful, landmark book, The Rape of Nanking: The Forgotten Holocaust of World War II. She single-handedly brought to world attention one of the most tragic, but least known, chapters of World War II: the slaughter, rape and torture of over 300,000 captive, disarmed Chinese soldiers and civilians by Japanese soldiers in the then capital of China in December 1937 and in the early months of 1938. "One of history's worst atrocities might have remained little more than a footnote had it not been for Iris Chang" (Reader's Digest, September 1, 1998)

The "Rape of Nanking" has also been an important force for the current international movement to put pressure on the Government of Japan to acknowledge and apologize for its wartime acts of systematic bestiality.

Iris Chang took her own life at age 36, while researching for a book about Japan's inhumane treatment of POWs. ◆

IRIS CHANG ON THE COVER OF READER'S DIGEST, SEPTEMBER, 1998. THE COVER READS, "SHE DIDN'T FORGET"

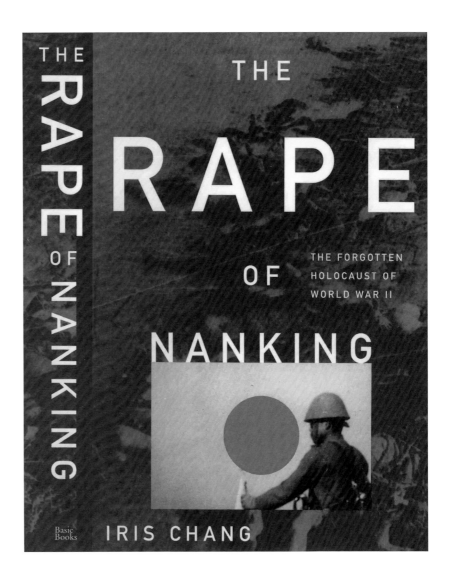

THE COVER OF IRIS CHANG'S MOST FAMOUS
BOOK — "THE RAPE OF NANKING" (1997).

A Speech by
Iris Chang

Addressed at the University Laboratory High School (of the University of Illinois) graduation in acceptance of the Max Beberman Award in 1998.

"One person can make an enormous difference in the world. One person actually, one idea can start a war, or end one, or subvert an entire power structure. One discovery can cure a disease or spawn new technology to benefit or annihilate the human race. You as one individual can change millions of lives."

You're going to find that we live in a world in which international law has much less to do with actual justice than international politics and money, a world in which not just thousands but hundreds of thousands of people, millions, even, can be slaughtered and then forgotten only a few decades later, a world in which those who have power often believe that they're above the truth and can distort the truth as if the truth itself is negotiable.

When I wrote the Rape of Nanking, I was shocked to see the extent to which genocide and bloodshed had stained the annals of world history. .And I was appalled not only by these stories but by the ease with which people forget them at the peril of civilization itself. The only thing that kept me going at times was the knowledge that a few people out there might be moved by the book including people still unborn, who might discover the story in their libraries, people who might work together to create a world in which horrors like the Rape of Nanking never happen again.

My greatest hope is that a few of you in this auditorium today will not be made cynical by the forces of greed, exploitation and corruption in our society, and that a few of you will actually cling to any desire you might have to serve as crusaders for truth, beauty and justice. People like that are needed to create a better world for the next generation of humankind on this planet and to ensure the survival of our civilization.

First of all, **please** believe in **the power of one**. One person can make an enormous difference in the world. One person actually, one **idea** can start a war, or end one, or subvert an entire power structure. One discovery can cure a disease or spawn new technology to benefit or annihilate the human race. You as **one** individual can change millions of lives. Think big. Do not limit your vision and do not **ever** compromise your dreams or ideals. You may find, in the end, that you are your own worst enemy. ♦

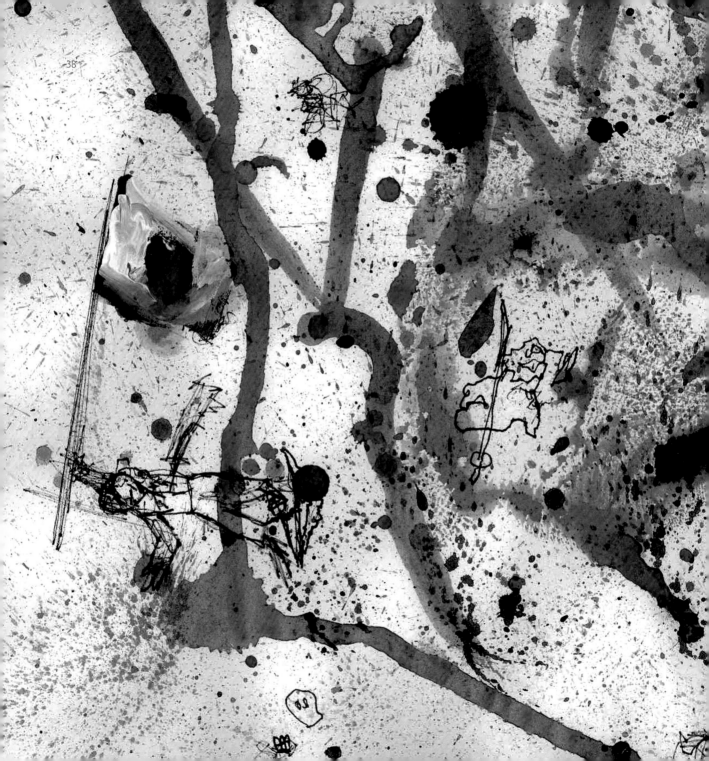

Kenny Chow, 13
THE FORGOTTEN MASSACRE WAS A TIME OF DEATHS AND BLOOD IN WW2
WITH THE JAPANESE'S ATTACK ON ASIA AND CHINA. MANY, MANY DEATHS OF
WOMEN AND CHILDREN CREATE ANGER IN EVERYONE'S HEARTS AND MIND.

Writing & Artwork

The Rape of Nanking:

A Quest for Peace

Essay Hann-Shuin Yew, 1st Prize winner

History is the discovering of the constant and universal principles of human nature.

— DAVID HUME

Truth, they tell us, is grey. It can be the grey of grainy old photographs, bitterly stark and bare. It can be the grey of the Nanjing Memorial Hall of Compatriots, stony in silent remembrance. It can be the grey of a bayonet blade, searing its way through a helpless infant. Or it can be the dull grey of clammy skin, the pallor of unsought death. In the Rape of Nanjing, there are many shades of grey. Each as true as the others.

I first came across Iris Chang's The Rape of Nanking when I was in fifth grade. At that point in time, the black and white of her pages frightened me, and I skittered to the gaily comfortable present without glancing back. In the years that passed, the massacre hovered in the back of my mind, quiescent but never quiet. For even through the hazy details, I had an irrepressible sense that evil had taken root in Nanjing from December 1937 to January 1938. Yet the issue was so volatile, the topic so raw that it could never be brought up in casual passing. I freely admit that I had no stirring cause to revisit Nanking. I rarely picked up the book and never finished it.

Until lions have their historians, tales of the hunt shall always glorify the hunters.

— AFRICAN PROVERTB

Not until two years ago, that is. When the monochrome of The Rape of Nanking was splashed anew with blood and the Rape claimed one more tragedy. Iris Chang's demise made it an obligation — no, made it necessary — for me to finally read The Rape of Nanking. I had to find the courage to face the horrors and the terrors she outlined so bleakly in her book.

Read. Recoil. Review and recoil again. I could not read that quietly and believe in its truth. While I too had lost relatives to the war, the tortures and atrocities of the Rape were so extreme they were unthinkable. How could I believe that people were that bestial? Despite the stark photographs and stacks of bibliographic sources in The Rape of Nanking, a part of me wanted to see matters from another angle, tame the fiery ghosts of a past I could not simply accept. I set myself a personal quest to find out more about the massacre — from another point of view.

A recent study conducted at Emory University located the physical basis for a psychological phenomenon termed the confirmation bias[1]. It is all too human to seek and find confirmatory evidence in support of already existing beliefs and ignore or reinterpret evidence to the contrary. This surety only widened the yawning abyss I soon found myself crisscrossing as I questioned both my Chinese and Japanese friends on their views of the Nanjing Massacre.

The issue literally exploded in my face. I had not realized how closely bitterness on both ends ran to the surface until I started searching for the scabs. I will never forget the one time a Japanese classmate joked, "Well, at least my grandparents beat your grandparents!" I had imagined that being two generations removed, we would be able to bring the topic out into open, civil discussion. Instead, some of my Japanese friends refused to comment on the subject, afraid to "offend" me because of my "Chineseness". In contrast, the Chinese spoke with passionate vitriol, lambasting the Japanese for their actions then and now. Even the Japanese classmates who agreed to talk to me about the matter bristled warily, strenuously pointing out that while the massacre did occur, the scale was "not as large as that claimed by the Chinese" and that the subject had been "blown out of proportion for political reasons" — all of which were echoed over and over as I searched the

Internet and libraries for more information. In fact, the Japanese felt almost as maligned as the Chinese! Friends on both sides sent me lists of websites and wrote detailed expostulations on their views, as I marveled at how blind I had been. Just how deep did this mutual resentment run? What was I doing, in my own small way, by bringing up the past — as Iris Chang had done? Most of all, would it ever end?

The most painful issue surrounding the Nanjing Massacre is arguably its lack of closure. Despite the Japanese view that World War II is long bygone, the fact remains that Japan has yet to make a mutually acceptable apology to the Chinese for its war actions[2]. Furthermore, as pointed out by Iris Chang, Japan has never come under strong international scrutiny — a fact which adds both to the atmosphere of denial that continues to pervade Japan and to the rancor of the Chinese.

When I first read The Rape of Nanking, I was incredulous that an entire nation could be so stubborn in its refusal to acknowledge the truth. After learning more about Japanese views on Nanjing, however, I learnt just how much truth is in the eye of the beholder. The Sino-Japanese impasse is not simply a matter of recalcitrance — but of self-martyrdom. To Japan, the recent clamor for justice is in part a political ploy by China to shame Japan on the world stage. With Japan on the defensive and beleaguered, will it ever truly apologize? Without an apology, can China forgive Japan?

This Gordian tangle makes it clear that the Nanjing Massacre requires global arbitration. As long as China remains the sole crier for justice, Japan will refuse to "give in", and Nanjing tensions will only continue to simmer, ready to erupt at the slightest provocation.

Another volcanic topic that inflames discussions of the massacre is the war over numbers, ranging from Japanese claims of 100 000 deaths to Chinese charges of 350 000 or more. It is almost as if a smaller number of deaths would justify the Japanese — or by extension, as if increasing the death toll adds to the righteousness of the Chinese. In the end, what does it matter exactly how many died? Even Stalin understood that our humanity disappears when death becomes a glut of

A stiff apology is a second insult…The injured party does not want to be compensated because he has been wronged; he wants to be healed because he has been hurt.

— G.K. CHESTERTON

statistics. It is simply not worthwhile to allow this issue to continue jeopardizing dialogue between China and Japan.

This current political climate has turned Nanjing into a smoking gun rather than a chance for catharsis. Whereas other massacres become opportunities for open, candid evaluation of humanity at its best and its worst, Nanjing is still swallowed up in unremitting strife decades later. In short, the Nanjing Massacre is not over yet — and will not be until it achieves its proper place in the past, rather than the present, of Chinese and Japanese consciousness.

The continuing contention over Nanjing poisons its own saga as well. I cannot help but feel that the tale of the Nanjing Massacre yearns for more than an ending. It is a tragedy not only of human lives, but of the human spirit — not only in what happened, but in how it could have happened. It is a tragedy not only for the Chinese, but for the Japanese military that allowed this to occur. Yet the extreme polarization and politicization of the bloodbath leaves little room for detached reflection. Every action on the part of either the Japanese or the Chinese is subject to protest, outrage and revulsion. Amidst the roiling mutual acrimony, is it possible to simply mourn the losses of the past?

My uncle was born in post-war China and raised in Singapore. He identifies himself fiercely as a Chinese, with a furious patriotism inextricably bound to harsh prejudice. To the best of my knowledge, he has never had sushi in his life. He will never step into a Japanese restaurant for as long as he lives, nor befriend any Japanese. Despite having come to understand the violent legacy born of the Nanjing Massacre, I cannot do the same. Although I do not condone the Japanese actions during and since World War II, neither can I support a demonization of the Japanese race as a whole. Prejudice and hatred are cyclic affairs, and as Gandhi noted, there are not enough eyes in this world to justify relentless retaliation.

In fact, the story of The Rape of Nanking transcends a litany of destruction. It is a grim reflection of the banality of evil, reminding us once more how thin the veneer

Have I not reason to lament, "What man has made of man?"

— WORDSWORTH

of civilization truly is. Today we have Darfur. Yesterday was Rwanda. Nanking, in that sense, is but another grey stain on the mosaic of human existence.

As an ethnic Chinese, the Nanjing Massacre resonates particularly with me. In a world where people continue to be tortured and killed because of their skin, even the most open-minded of us must acknowledge the boundaries of color and blood that divide humanity. Ironically, however, each gruesome genocide serves not to highlight, but rather to blur the distinctions between us. Nanjing hammers home the message that no race is better than any other. Today some may be tempted to look at war-torn Africa and judge her people as innately inferior beings, incapable of peaceful self-governance. Before doing so, however, we should stop and take stock. Hitler. Pol Pot. Milosevic. Saddam Hussein. Enver. Jamal. Talat. All of us are culpable. All of us are capable of submerging our moral sense beneath hatred and prejudice, a fact which should never be forgotten.

The other day I ran a simple web search for the words "Holocaust genocide" and found over 7.2 million entries. "Rwanda genocide", 7 million. "Darfur genocide", 7 million. "Bosnia genocide", 3.7 million. "Cambodia genocide", 2.4 million. "Nanking genocide". A mere one hundred thousand entries. Although the NanJing DaTuSha continues to burn in the consciousness of the Chinese and Japanese people, it receives minimal coverage in the Western world. Why?

"To forget a holocaust is to kill twice." More than anything, The Rape of Nanking must be commended for heeding Elie Wiesel's warning. With its clear descriptions and scrupulous detail, it has opened up a firestorm of controversy that is almost as valuable as the history it imparts. By bringing the saga of Nanjing into the English-speaking world, The Rape of Nanking refocused attention on this barely-buried past, taking the first of many steps towards achieving a much-needed sense of closure. After reading extensive scholarly Japanese refutations of aspects of this book, I have discovered just how hazy the truth can be. I cannot state with certainty that the Japanese rebuttals are completely groundless. Nevertheless, it is undeniable that without The Rape of Nanking, few without an immediate connection to either China or Japan would have heard of this terrible episode. Including me.

Words are the means to meaning, and for some, the annunciation of truth.

— G.K. CHESTERTON

Seventy years have passed since the Nanjing Massacre, and yet its legacy remains raw. The scars of World War II still serve as emotional rallying points for patriotism — and mutual hostility. For Chinese worldwide, Nanjing is not only a potent cry for justice, but a channel for national pride — even at the cost of strong anti-Japanese sentiment. As a result, Japan's war past has become even more inextricably tied to the delicate question of its national identity. For until Japan can give a coherent and globally acceptable response to the question of war responsibility, its former aggression will only continue to perpetuate resentment within the rest of Asia. Just as Germany will always bring to mind the Holocaust, Japan will always be remembered as a perpetrator of crimes against Asia, a fact it cannot hope to whitewash or understate. By regaining the acceptance of its Asian neighbors, Japan will not only recapture its own cultural identity[3], but earn the respect so central to its values.

In Singapore, we call it "Sook Ching". It was a month-long systematic extermination of Chinese Singaporeans and Malayans by the Japanese military administration during World War II, ostensibly to eliminate 'hostile' elements. Thousands of Chinese men were machine-gunned or drowned, with the killing only ending when Japan's military resources thinned from employment elsewhere. It is not known how many died, though accepted estimates range around 50 000. The episode echoes Hitler's "Final Solution" in its cold-blooded purpose. Find, assemble and eliminate.

"Sook Ching" means "cleansing purge", and is a corollary to the atrocities Japan committed within China. Its smaller scope does not render it any less of a crime than the Nanjing Massacre, and as with its larger cousin, there is still no official apology from Japan to Singapore for this war crime[4]. Yet Sook Ching is a forgotten holocaust within the 'forgotten holocaust'. Even within the Chinese community, it is generally relegated to a hurried byline. Worse, in Singapore history books, the Sook Ching massacre rarely takes up more than a paragraph or two, a page at most. Searching the web turns up few sources and even fewer references to primary records. As a Chinese Singaporean, I was stunned to discover what a blank slate

The value of identity of course is that so often with it comes purpose.

— RICHARD R. GRANT

History, despite its wrenching pain, cannot be unlived, but if faced with courage, need not be lived again.

— MAYA ANGELOU

Sook Ching was. I wonder if this was how Iris Chang felt when she first started searching for resources for The Rape of Nanking. It is frightening, to have to ask oneself where the history of fifty thousand innocents is.

In some ways, the story of Sook Ching is an even greater tragedy than that of Nanjing. Though the furious contention over Nanjing is distressing, the fact remains that there is discussion, however rancorous, taking place. The questions of responsibility, morality and humanity that the Nanjing Massacre raises are timeless, and ought to be applied to Sook Ching. Singapore is a young nation, and Sook Ching arguably the one large-scale crime against humanity that has taken place in its past. It would not hurt Singapore or Singaporeans to delve into this soul-searching tragedy. After all, in forgetting history we not only are doomed to repeat it. We do a disservice to those who lived and died in it. ♦

1 Shermer, Michael. "Skeptic: The Political Brain." Scientific American July 2006: 36.

2 Yamaguchi, Mari. "Japan's Apology Breaks No New Ground." Associated Press. China Daily 22 Apr 2005. World. July 18 2006. http://www.chinadaily.com.cn/english/doc/2005-04/22/content_436701.htm

3 Togo, Kazuhiko. "A Moratorium on Yasukuni Visits." Far Eastern Economic Review June 2006 July 19 2006 http://www.feer.com/articles1/2006/0606/free/p005.html .

4 Kwok, Wai Keng. "Justice Done? Criminal and Moral Responsibility Issues in the Chinese Massacres Trial, Singapore, 1947." Working paper, electronic version. 2001. Yale University Genocide Studies Program. July 19 2006 http://www.yale.edu/gsp/publications/WaiKeng.doc .

An essay to raise awareness of the importance of

Remembrance of History

Essay Graeme A. Stacey, 2nd Prize winner

"Because of Iris Chang… I now embrace the notion that one person can make a difference."

Iris Chang's effort to expose the 1937 story of Japanese atrocities in Nanking has impacted me personally through the realization that such historic events are both contemporary and relevant to today's fight for justice and truth. I have been so motivated by the personal advocating of Chang's beliefs that I am more sensitive to human rights; they are now a key factor in what I teach high school students. The media bombards us daily with injustice and tragedy because our freedom of expression allows the media to do so. Similarly, our freedom of expression allows us to act on these injustices unlike the limitations placed on oppressed victims. Because of Iris Chang's The Rape of Nanking: The Forgotten Holocaust Of World War II, her accompanying speeches, radio and television appearances, I now embrace the notion that one person can make a difference. I feel strongly that students in today's classrooms need to know this. Not to teach this is dangerous because victims of atrocities, such as those at Nanking, do not live forever; there-fore, their stories must. Otherwise, perpetrators go unaccountable and the tangible link between history and current events becomes diminished.

Throughout high school, college, university, and as a student teacher, I was taught very little about the Asia Pacific theater of war. Why had I not been exposed to this? It depicts the inhumanity, death, and torture faced by innocent civilians and brave soldiers, highlighting the inhumanity that is repeated throughout history. Iris Chang's book immediately opened for me a previously unknown chapter of his-tory. It was history, as stated by Stephan Ambrose, that Chang understood needed to be communicated in an interesting way (The Australian). After reading her book I made a professional and personal commitment to expose this contemporary and historic chapter of history. As a high school social studies teacher, my curriculum responsibilities relate to twentieth century world history and historical / contempo-rary Canadian history. I have molded my studies, interests, and pursuits in this field in order to become a "specialist." I came about the Rape of Nanking by chance, almost incidentally. I have a passionate interest in Canadian Hong Kong Veterans who served in defense of the British crown colony of Hong Kong, only to spend close to four years as prisoners of the Japanese Imperial Army. The Canadian Hong Kong Veterans' experiences as prisoners lacked exposure in Canada, yet they are stories that fit within the events associated with the Japanese plans for a Greater East Asian Co-Prosperity Sphere.

In British Columbia high school classrooms, the story of the Asia-Pacific, specifi-cally the rape of Nanking, is not told in any significant detail. Why? Is it shame over the Canadian governments' actions regarding our Hong Kong Veterans? Is it accountability factors or fears of offending a valuable trading partner in Japan? Is the silence of veterans and civilian victims a result of their many years of neglect? In the case of the Asia Pacific War, there are limited available resources for British Columbia teachers. Traditionally, Canadian textbooks have focused on the Euro-pean theater of WWII. It is Iris Chang's book that inspired me, between 1999 – 2001, to get involved with the British Columbia Ministry of Education and the B.C. Asso-

"Iris Chang's book immediately opened for me a previously unknown chapter of history."

"This resource, complete with an introduction, teacher backgrounder, five lessons on the Asia Pacific (lesson two being the "Nanking Massacre and other Atrocities"), resources and handouts, became available in 2003 to all senior social studies teachers in the province of British Columbia. "

ciation for Learning & Preserving the History of WWII in Asia (Alpha) to create a resource guide for teachers to support aspects of the senior social studies curriculum: Human Rights in the Asia Pacific 1931–1945: Social Responsibility And Global Citizenship. This resource, complete with an introduction, teacher backgrounder, five lessons on the Asia Pacific (lesson two being the "Nanking Massacre and other Atrocities"), resources and handouts, became available in 2003 to all senior social studies teachers in the province of British Columbia. Among other rationales for such a resource is the premise that, "If we break the cycle of violence, humankind must constantly remind itself of its own capacity for evil, more importantly, must educate itself on how to prevent crimes against humanity" (Human Rights in the Asia Pacific 1931–1945, p. 4). It is my hope that this subject may follow "a trend…also [be a] beginning that will require American schoolchildren to learn about the rape of Nanking as part of their history curriculum" (Contemporary Authors, p. 2). Imagine the way Chang presents the Nanking massacre, with primary source accounts and oral narratives from survivors and witnesses, as opposed to the "…dry compilation of statistics" (Contemporary Authors, p. 2) found in textbook. This is evident with History 12 students' responses to Chang's version of the 1937 events: "I was disgusted!" (Rhys Myhannis, 2006); "It's a pity we don't learn more about it" (Richard Combs, 2006); "…said to be like the Holocaust, but I found it more depressing with the rapes and torture methods inflicted upon civilians" (Kyla Pierson, 2006); "It reminds me of stories my mom told me …my great-grandmother and grandma hid in a cave during the Japanese occupation of the Philippines. I would have liked to know more because this part of history affected my family" (Sarika Kelm, 2006). Students like Sarika do know more, and in doing so, empower the memory of the victims. Ms. Chang stated in 1998, "…denial and amnesia are considered to be part of the final stage of genocide. First, the victims are killed, and then the memory of killing itself is killed" (Siegel). In my senior social studies classes, this is not going to happen!

Iris Chang was not afraid to take a risk with what others thought; she was driven by a conviction to expose a horrible truth. Her objectives were clear;

"I wrote [the story] out of a sense of rage. I didn't really care if I made a cent from it. It was important to me that the world knew what happened in Nanking back in 1937" (The Australian, p. 2). As I learned of the tragedies and the horrors of war, and the true meaning of genocide as experienced by the Nanking victims, I started to develop the confidence needed to take risks like Chang did. After participating in the creation of "Human Rights in the Asia Pacific 1931– 1945: Social Responsibility And Global Citizenship" I decided to propose a course for high school students on genocide that would use the Holocaust as a blueprint or starting point to engage students. I was careful however in my planning "not to attempt to show that one ethnic group's suffering was worse than another" (Contemporary Authors, p. 2). Genocide does not appear in any specific curriculum (beyond a definition which is void of what victims endure), although elements of what genocide is are touched on in various high school courses. My motivation in creating the course was two-fold. First I wanted to learn more about these topics myself. If I was just scratching the surface of grand scale historic and contemporary examples of tragedy and injustice, my students would have a similarly superficial understanding. My second motivation was that I wanted to teach my students of such events in a way that surpassed the simplified, scaled down version found in a textbook. In 2003 I took a risk; I proposed a course that would study genocide. I presented "Holocaust 12: A Blueprint for Modern Societal Tragedies" to School District #23's (Central Okanagan) board of trustees, administrators, and superintendents. No course of this kind, to my knowledge or to the knowledge of the board, had ever been taught at the public school level in our province. It was risky in terms of the impact it could have on students, and the public's reaction, as well as the possibility of naysayers within and without the school to such a course. My biggest concern however was whether students would register for such a specific course and how I would develop curriculum for such a sensitive topic? Since its inception, the course has grown from one semestered course to three for the 2006 / 2007 school year at Mount Boucherie Secondary. The Holocaust is studied as an example to further understand other genocides such as the rape of Nanking (Japanese Imperial Army), Cambodia (Pol Pot), Rwanda (Hutu

"In 2003 I took a risk; I proposed a course that would study genocide."

It wasn't so much the sheer numbers as the details that shock — fathers forced at gunpoint to rape daughters, stakes driven through vaginas, women nailed to trees, tied-up prisoners used for bayonet practice, breasts sliced off the living, speed decapitation contest.

Perpetrators), Yugoslavia (Slobodan Milosevic), and modern Darfur. Thus students are able to draw comparisons and contrast these events.

A key aspect of my course is hope and selfless action. It is examined in the lives of heroes who have acted in the face of danger and tyranny. Such heroes are presented as examples for students to follow in their daily lives. They have acted on their learned knowledge by writing provincially recognized award winning essays such as "Genocide: The Paroxysm Of Human Hatred" by Jen Rekis, and "The Relevance of Night Today", by Tanya Armes. Students also write letters to survivors, as well as to various media publications in order to inform the public. This way their knowledge can make a difference in places like Sudan and Rwanda. My students have warned of hate, fundraised for women's shelters and Sudanese refugees with, for example the sale of T-shirts, one titled, "Give Hate a Break" another "Stop Genocide in Sudan". These "mini-activists" are making a difference. Like Iris Chang, I share a "…pride in breaking the silence…comparing [the Holocaust and] the rape of Nanking to more recent brutality in Bosnia, Rwanda…" (Siegel, p.2).

Beyond hope and selfless action in the face of hate I have my students focus on the four basic groups of individuals associated with the Holocaust and other genocides: bystanders, victims, perpetrators, and heroes / saviors. Students study these four types throughout Holocaust 12 and are able to identify each. Students understand and are aware of the concept of hate and its impact at a personal and societal level. At the conclusion of this course, students are able to identify these concepts and relate them to events both historic and contemporary, while gaining awareness and assessing critical problems in our society. This empowers students to make a difference. In the words of one of my students at the conclusion of taking Holocaust 12: A Blueprint for Modern Societal Tragedies, "I have learned about the darkest times in human civilization. I have come to see the darkness of the human heart, but not just because of the atrocities we have committed but because of the lack of action taken…because of this class we will never be bystanders, we will be saviors". At the conclusion of this course, a greater

By bringing the story to the public realm, the fight for justice and truth is brought to a forum where it can't be hidden.

number of students each year are armed and educated about human disaster. Some critics have questioned my motives, stating these are "only students," seventeen or eighteen years old. Their age however is a benefit because they are future leaders and they will carry this knowledge with them. I know they make a difference; I have seen it, especially when compared to "…a world in which so many international figures — the United Nations' Kofi Annan immediately comes to mind — seem content to deal with the challenge of human disaster in the fashion of athletes out to achieve a winning record (you may lose in Rwanda, but you win East Timor)" (Mills, p. 40). My students, like Chang have a moral integrity that set them apart.

The denial and dismissal of blatant, malicious, and purposeful genocide, if listened to by an apathetic audience is dangerous. If not challenged such denial aids the perpetrator in denying victims their suffering even further. People are impressionable, especially hearing something for the first time. Some of the most impressionable are students who are easily swayed and often won't challenge what they are told regarding required curriculum. For the rape of Nanking to be called an "unfortunate incident" does not serve justice. Consider:

Over a six-week period, up to 80,000 women were raped. But it wasn't so much the sheer numbers as the details that shock — fathers forced at gunpoint to rape daughters, stakes driven through vaginas, women nailed to trees, tied-up prisoners used for bayonet practice, breast sliced off the living, speed decapitation contest (August, p. 1).

Is this a mere "unfortunate incident?" Iris Chang sets the bar high when challenging deniers. She went as far as challenging the Japanese ambassador to America to apologize for the Nanking Massacre, calling into question the integrity of the Japanese government. Bringing the story to the public realm, the fight for justice and truth is brought to a forum where it can't be hidden. Exposure of events is a method of combating denial. Teaching a high school course that identifies perpetrators and incorporates the truth of genocide in all social studies courses will make a difference in combating both silent and not so silent critics. Iris

Chang has faced great deniers. Nobukatsu Fujioka, a right wing commentator, openly campaigned to prevent publication of her book in Japan by citing errors. He also published a book denouncing Chang as a propagandist funded by Japan-haters (August, p. 3). What is most disheartening for me, as an individual who wants to make a difference, is to hear that Japanese right-wingers interpreted her suicide as belated support for their contention that the massacre never happened (August, p. 4). Never happened? My students will know it happened, as will my colleagues, my family and friends, and their family and friends. The rape of Nanking is a distinct, yet unfortunately common, injustice that Iris Chang brought to the "public's consciousness" (Ramzy, p.14).

Many people have inspired, influenced, and challenged me as an educator: Canadian Hong Kong Veterans who spent close to four years in prisoner of war camps and can now tell their stories without hate; Dr. Leon Bass, a black American educator, racism and holocaust consultant who inspires with his message that intolerance is not acceptable; Madiom a five-year-old southern Sudanese boy with a brilliant smile — despite his 7.4kg skeletal body, emaciated by hunger; and my students who, despite their complicated, confusing, and issues-filled lives, show up every day with a desire to learn. But of all these people, it was Iris Chang who first taught me to be aware, aware with the intention to make a difference. I am one of "…the millions of people whom she touched through her writings and her activism…promoting peace between peoples of different races and backgrounds" (Benson). I will continue to keep her memory and mission alive in my life and in my classroom so that she does not become yet another victim of the Rape of Nanking. ♦

Never happened? My students will know it happened, as will my colleagues, my family and friends, and their family and friends. The rape of Nanking is a distinct, yet unfortunately common, injustice.

August, Oliver. "One Final Victim of the Rape of Nanking?" Times, The 17 Mar. 2005. Newspaper Source. EBSCO. 8 May 2006 http://search.epnet.com.

Benson, Heidi. "LOS ALTOS 600 Mourn Death of Best-Selling Author Iris Chang, 36, 'achieved enough for many lifetimes.'" San Francisco Chronicle (CA) 11 Nov. 2004. Newspaper Source. EBSCO. 8 May 2006 http://search. epnet.com.

Contemporary Authors Online: Iris Chang. Farmington Hills: Thomson Gale, 2006. Contemporary Authors. Thomson Gale. 8 May 2006 http://infotrac.galegroup.com.

"Fragile Chronicler of Japanese Invasion Atrocities." The Australian 17 Nov. 2004. Newspaper Source. EBSCO. 8 May 2006 http://search.epnet.com .

Human Rights in the Asia Pacific 1931–1945: Social Responsibility and Global Citizenship. British Columbia Ministry of Education, 2002. 8 May 2006.

"Iris Chang; To Come." The Economist (US) 27 Nov. 2004. InfoTrac K-12 Series. Thomson Gale. 8 May 2006 http://infotrac.galegroup.com.

Jenkins, Russell. "The Rape of Nanking: The Forgotten Holocaust of World War II." National Review 10 Nov. 1997. InfoTrac K-12 Series. Thomson Gale. 8 May 2006 http://infotrac.galegroup.com.

Un-forgetting

Essay Adeline Oka, 3rd Prize winner

"Those who cannot remember the past are condemned to repeat it"

— GEORGE SANTAYANA

In writing The Rape of Nanking, Iris Chang so wisely heeded the words of George Santayana: "Those who cannot remember the past are condemned to repeat it" (16). This classic lesson, so thoroughly presented in school, was absent from my home and family discourses. For reasons I am still trying to discover, history was seldom discussed and subsequently the silence on the subject implied its irrelevance in our family's affairs. Instead, my parents instilled in me the value of the future. "You are an outsider," they would say. "You must prove yourself." They sought to equip me to succeed—economically and socially—in my future in America. Ironically, it was the lack of a connection with my own history that blocked true acclimation into American society. Whereas my peers easily articulated their heritages in precise mathematical terms—one friend prided herself on being a quarter Irish, one-eighth German, one-eighth Norwegian, one-tenth Native American, and the rest "American"—I struggled to publicly acknowledge the one simple fact that I was born in Indonesia, let alone my more complex Chinese heritage, for I did not understand my cultural identity. Yet I've realized that to dodge the very problems that caused my parents and grandparents to avoid their past, it was and is imperative to acknowledge and understand those problems in the first place. Doing so requires learning history, accepting it, and ultimately speaking out about it.

As a member of the diasporic Chinese community, I found Ms. Chang's book to be a beacon of light in the dark seas of self-discovery. Her work is groundbreaking in its study of Sino-Japanese relations in the twentieth century, but is even

"While Ms. Chang's words have made an indelible impact in my academic development, the biggest change she has made in my life has been enabling me to find my own words. History is not distant; it is personal."

more revealing in its study of cultural memory. While Ms. Chang's words have made an indelible impact in my academic development, the biggest change she has made in my life has been enabling me to find my own words. History is not distant; it is personal. Her thoughtful reflections have inspired me, not so much to dig deep into my past, but rather to take note of what was apparent but was unspoken.

I first became acquainted with the atrocities of Nanking ten years ago in Chinese school. Having been inspired by my great-aunt, the prolific linguist who in her seventies decided to take up Mandarin, I chose to enroll in Chinese school. Up to that point in my life, my only understanding of my Chinese background was the knowledge that my family was Chinese. What that meant exactly, I did not know. Neither my parents nor grandparents spoke, wrote, or read a single character of Mandarin. We had no relatives who were born in China. We were neither Buddhists nor members of any prominent Chinese religion, nor did we celebrate any Chinese holidays.

In spite of what I saw to be a clear and obvious estrangement from China, I grew up learning "Chinese" values. My grandmother would always say, "You are not like these Americans. You are different. You must be proper; you are Chinese." But at Chinese school, I realized just how un-Chinese I was. My classmates believed I was dim-witted for not understanding the teacher's instructions. My teachers, on the other hand, believed I was a rebellious child: they viewed my inability to speak Chinese as a form of disrespect or, at best, an indicator of being uncultured. I began to see myself as a cultural non-entity. In Indonesia the Chinese were persecuted. Here in the Chinese community, I found myself an outsider yet again.

When I learned about the Nanking massacre, I was moved to act. I forgot about my feelings of awkwardness amid the Chinese community and became active in promoting awareness of the Rape. I no longer cared about being an outsider, but saw myself as part of a larger movement for justice. I spoke out in my middle school, urging my American classmates and teachers to sign petitions that called for reparations to be paid to Nanking victims. In a strange way, the culture of oppression unites people. Iris Chang writes, "There are several important lessons to be learned from Nanking, and one is that civilization itself is tissue-thin" (220). In learning about the exploitation of others, we are reminded of our own vulnerability — and ultimately, our humanity.

"I read the [Iris Chang's] book ... Instead of becoming apathetic, I became pro-active."

Three years ago my interest in Nanking resurfaced when I took a college class on Asian Civilization. I decided to read Chang's book, but was skeptical about it. I felt that the more atrocities I was exposed to, the more desensitized I would become and this would only result in my becoming apathetic to injustice. But what I expected to be a sensationalized account of a regional war turned out to be one of the most important texts I would read in my college years. I read the book to satisfy an academic curiosity, but the experience became for me, as it was for Ms. Chang, "a personal exploration into the shadow side of human nature" (220). Instead of becoming apathetic, I became pro-active. I personally investigated, starting with questioning my grandmother. A retired instructor of the German language, my grandmother is an accomplished, educated, woman of the world. Yet whenever I ask her about our family history, she derides my efforts, dismisses my queries as pointless digs at the past, and rhetorically asks me why I was so weird. Wondering if the horrors of Nanking were duplicated in Indonesia, I asked her about the era of Japanese occupation. She recalled that those were hard times.

"We had no lights," she began. "We could only use oil or gas lamps. If any household used electric lights, the soldiers would pound loudly on the doors and shout 'Lights! Lights!' We also did not have shoes in that era. Many people went around covered only in [I imagine burlap] rice sacks. We were forbidden to eat white rice; all white rice was reserved for the military. We could only eat an inferior type of reddish-brown rice or a concoction of the cheap rice with cornmeal. If we had any white rice we had to sneak around to eat it because we never knew what the Japanese would do to us if we were caught. There were reports of men being captured by the Japanese, stores looted, and women being raped. The Japanese often snatched single women and took them as their wives." I asked her if she witnessed any violence first-hand. "No," she said. "My sisters and I stayed indoors all the time [during those years]. We were too afraid to come outside."

I asked her if there was much discussion about the Nanking horrors when she was growing up. At first she did not know what I was talking about. When I explained, she remembered a time, long before the Japanese occupation of Indonesia, when there were newspaper reports of the war between Japan and China. "My mother was very interested in the war. She followed the newspaper stories diligently. She kept a tally of the war casualties in the Bible." I asked my grandmother if she still had those records. She told me she did not. "But what did it matter, it was only numbers." I imagine that it was not from insensitivity to the Nanking massacre that my grandmother uttered that remark; rather, it was reflective of an attitude that my grandmother, and many others have about the value of history. For many people, especially those who are fortunate to have escaped horrific pasts, history is only a series of numbers, of names and dates. We can turn to religion or philosophy, perhaps even economics, for the solutions to our existential plights. Not history.

I asked my grandmother about the post-war years. I had one sole motive for asking this question: to understand my family background and the persecution from which they escaped. Growing up, my parents constantly reminded me of my place in society. "You are a minority," they would say. Yet growing up in Los Angeles, I sensed a disequilibrium between what I was taught in my home and what I experienced outside of it, namely, that there were no minorities in this pluralistic community. For years I just assumed that my parents were paranoid, but as I grew up and learned about the second-class status of the Chinese in Indonesia, I began to understand my parents', sometimes defensive, attitudes. I had felt, for years, that my family was petty and even a bit racist, when they made distinctions between the native Indonesians and the Chinese, emphasizing that we belonged strictly in the category of the latter. I, for one, could not even distinguish between a native Indonesian and a Chinese-Indonesian. My worldview was lacking a historical understanding, and consequently I felt disconnected from the world of my relatives.

"I had come to understand why there were tensions between the Chinese and Japanese and hoped that I would be able to extrapolate on these tensions and apply them to my own cultural history."

When I learned about Nanking, I wondered if Indonesian persecution against the Chinese was in any way linked to resentment towards Japan for wartime atrocities. I had come to understand somewhat why there were tensions between the Chinese and Japanese and hoped that I would be able to extrapolate on these tensions and apply them to my own cultural history. All my grandmother would say was that after the war, everyone did their best to get back on their feet. "We were grateful when we could feed our families," she said. "There was no more talk of Japan." But how could all those people so easily dismiss what happened in Nanking and in Indonesia? I asked her. Was there no more fear? Or hate? My grandmother told me that hate would always be there. "We cannot see what lays buried deep inside people's hearts," she said. Yet she made it clear that there were no discussions about the war, in Nanking or in Indonesia, and that the focus for the Chinese-Indonesian families was to make progress in their situations and plan for the future. The past was to be left in the bookshelves, in notes left in Bibles like that belonging to great-grandmother.

In recent years there has been increased violence against the Chinese population perpetrated by native Indonesians. My mother explained, that while resentment for the Japanese occupation of Indonesia (acted out towards the Japanese resembling Chinese) may have contributed to this persecution, ultimately the hatred towards the Chinese is an economic, not a racial or political, problem. In Indonesia, the Chinese wield the majority of the commercial power. They are merchants, investors, and entrepreneurs, living in an environment of extreme poverty. I couldn't help but draw parallels to the Jewish bankers who were scapegoated for Europe's financial troubles in the pre-war years. I mentioned this observation to my mother, suggesting that the parallels between the two situations proved the need to study history, even in matters that seemed purely economic. She told me that those who still have unfilled bellies will not be interested in history.

"Forgetting about one's past is a form of narcotic … Unfortunately, we cannot escape history. It remains with us in the present and follows us into the future."

Chang makes clear that she does not see the Japanese as an inherently violent race. While some experts affirm the innate aggression of certain cultures, no matter how sophisticated they've become, for Chang, "there is an inherent danger in this assumption, for it has two implications: one, that the Japanese, by virtue of their religion, are naturally less humane than Western cultures and must be judged by different standards (an implication…both irresponsible and condescending), and two, that Judeo-Christian cultures [to which my family subscribed] are somehow less capable of perpetrating atrocities like the Rape of Nanking" (55). A lack of historical understanding of horrors such as the Nanking massacre is likely to dismiss the event as a mere outgrowth of Japanese war culture. To attribute hate and violence as merely elements of human nature without looking to the social and historical contexts that have shaped particular instances of violence is to set humanity up for more.

Even after the actual "Rape" of Nanking ceased, the Japanese continued to subjugate the Chinese through promoting opium use, which was intended to "encourage addiction and further enslave the people…Many of the downtrodden citizens of Nanking fell prey to drugs because it gave them the means to escape, if only temporarily, from the misery of their lives" (163). Opium was used to both pacify the people as well as to oppress them. In a similar manner, forgetting about one's past is a form of narcotic, a means of coping and escaping. Unfortunately, we cannot escape history. It remains with us in the present and follows us into the future.

"The Rape of Nanking was not simply an event that took place in a war a long time ago; rather, it, like other manifestations of injustice, was a crime against humanity."

In the concluding pages of The Rape, Chang describes what that future is: the descendants of Nanking, whether by blood or by culture. She writes, "The American public is growing demographically more Asian. And unlike their parent, whose careers were heavily concentrated in scientific fields, the younger generations of Chinese Americans and Chinese Canadians are fast gaining influence in law, politics, and journalism — professions historically underrepresented by Asians in North America" (223). Ultimately the study of history looks to find solutions to humanity's problems. For my grandparents' and parents', this solution was principally economic. They struggled through discrimination in Indonesia, then financial hardship in America, in order to provide food for our bellies. For second-and third-generation Asian Americans, the elementary solution — i. e. economic stability — has already been put in place. It is time for us to work towards the social and political solutions. For me this means learning about history and speaking out against injustice.

I have spent the majority of my youth unsure of who I was and where I belonged. I wasn't quite Chinese, or Indonesian, or American. After I read The Rape of Nanking, I realized that historical awareness was indeed very significant to understanding one's identity amid cultural ambiguity. Iris Chang warns us time and time again that silence (in the face of oppression) is a form of consent. In my personal life, I have begun to tackle the silence of my parents and grandparents regarding our history, hoping to unravel the conspiracy, which, unbeknownst to them, they are party to. I have become more relentless in asking them about our ancestors from China: who were they? Why did they leave China? In my professional life, I have decided to become a voice for the voiceless, for victims of oppression. The Rape of Nanking was not simply an event that took place in a war a long time ago; rather, it, like other manifestations of injustice, was a crime against humanity. The exploitation of young women by the military in particular struck a chord in me. I began to study different forms of sexual exploitation, digging beneath the surface to understand the power structures that create prostitution. My studies have led me to my current job: working at a Los Angeles-based non-profit shelter and service provider for child victims of prostitution. For the kids I work with, for my parents and grandparents, for immigrants, and for all of humanity, the future holds the possibility of progress. I've learned from Ms. Chang, that progress cannot happen without understanding. And understanding cannot happen without remembering. ◆

70 Years of Amnesia — The Rape of Nanking

A POEM BY FLORA CHONG

In the expanse of time and space,
70 years went by like a breath

Sunrise and sunset
Tides high and low,
Life and death intertwine
People pass by
Without a slightest expression, a
twinkle in their eyes.

The killing, the bloodshed, the fear,
and the devilish acts
The truth too brutal, the suffering
too remote
Tears unseen, cries unheard
People fell into a collective amnesia

In a human heart made of flesh
70 years of unspeakable pain

Dark and hopeless,
Torturing memories and despair;
Living day by day
With a frail body, and a broken soul.

The killing, the bloodshed, the fear,
and the devilish acts;
The truth too brutal,
the suffering too close;
Tears unseen, cries unheard,
They fell into endless nightmares

Could we hear the voiceless cries?
Could we listen to their untold stories?
Did we see their tearful eyes?
Did we touch their bleeding hearts?

When would our souls awake, our
conscience yearn?
When could we speak loud and clear,
And give them our words?
Your stories will be told, your wound
will be healed;
Your soul will be comforted
The truth will prevail.

「南京大屠殺」令我看到人性最扭曲最殘暴的一面。張純如的出現才
讓我對人的本性重拾信心。然而，每當想起過去七十年、十四億中國
人竟然可以忍心把這個沉重的歷史包袱放在這個年青女孩子身上。我
感到非常痛心。我們的沉默不單使她成為另一位「南京大屠殺」的受
害者，更令這個尚在淌血的歷史傷口永遠無法癒合。

Iris practised what she preached: "Believe the power of one" . Her book, 'The Rape of Nanking',
changed the course of history . The horrific account of the story of the Rape is directly and
indirectly helping turn the tide of global opinion against the Japanese history revisionists.

In a sea of darkness when Evil ruled, Iris'courage and conviction for justice gave the world a
glimpse of hope that truth about Nanking would be unearthed and justice would prevail again.

Iris gave us a ray of hope. Let us continue her legacy and light up the rest of the world.

Dr. Joseph Y. K. Wong, C.M.

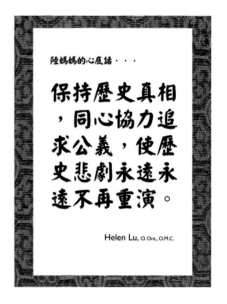

陸媽媽的心底話···

保持歷史真相
，同心協力追
求公義，使歷
史悲劇永遠永
遠不再重演。

Helen Lu, O. Ont., O.M.C.

Alanna Tai, 15

THE LOSS AND DECEPTION, THE SCREAMS, THE
CRIES…THE VIVID MEMORIES OF THE VICTIMS OF
THE NANKING MASSACRE HAVE ECHOED INTO
THE CHILDREN OF THE FUTURE. EVEN TODAY, THE
TRAGEDIES OF NANKING MASSACRE REMAIN IN
THE HEARTS OF MANY PEOPLE. READING ABOUT
IT TODAY, IT SEEMS ALMOST IMPOSSIBLE. THE SAD
TRUTH IS, IT ALL HAPPENED, AND THE SORROWS
SHOULD NEVER BE FORGOTTEN…BURNING
IMAGES IN MY MIND. THEY WILL BE REMEMBERED!

Vivian Hui, 17
THOSE WHO HAVE BEEN SILENCED IN PAIN
SHOULD BE GIVEN THE CHANCE TO SPEAK
ABOUT THE TRUTH. LET'S UNCOVER THE PAST
AND STOP THE SILENCE.

Linna Xu, 19
PORTAIT OF A 'COMFORT WOMAN'

Stephanie Kan, 18

THE FEMALE VICTIMS OF THE NANKING MASSACRE WERE ALL NORMAL WOMEN — NO DIFFERENT FROM THE WOMEN TODAY. AS A YOUNG WOMEN, I HAVE SO MANY DREAMS, SO MUCH I HAVEN'T ACCOMPLISHED. FOR THOSE VICTIMS TO BE FORCED TO MAKE A LIFE OR DEATH DECISION, AND BE MADE SEX SLAVES FOR CHOOSING LIFE, IS OUTRAGEOUS. THE JAPANESE TOOK AWAY SO MANY DREAMS WHEN THEY RAPED THOSE GIRLS. THE GIRLS WILL NEVER HAVE THE SAME LIVES AGAIN. THE WILL BE FOREVER LABELED AS 'DIRTY' AND 'VILE', BECAUSE THEY HAVE BEEN "COMFORT WOMEN FOR THE MONSTERS — THE OUTRAGEOUS JAPANESE SOLDIERS.

Chloe Leung, 13
WHY SO MUCH DARKNESS? A DROP OF
BLOOD IS A DROP OF TEAR.

Michelle Si, 15
LIFE IS A GIFT FROM GOD AND THE GREAT-
EST GIFT FOR MANKIND. DON'T DESTROY IT
FOR POWER!

Leon Tse, 13
ALWAYS REMEMBER THE VICTIMS AND NEVER
FORGET THOSE WHO CAUSED THE HORROR.

Angela Galang, 13

AS A FILIPINO-CANADIAN, I FEEL REALLY
SHOCKED AND ANGRY, WHEN ONE DAY I READ
A TEXT BOOK ABOUT THE "COMFORT WOMEN*"
FROM CHINA, KOREA, TAIWAN, PHILIPPINES,
DUTCH EAST INDIES... WOMEN AREN'T SUPPOSED
TO BE USED FOR PLEASURE OR EMBARRASSMENT.
THEY WEREN'T MADE FOR THIS! WE SHOULD
ALL MAKE AN EFFORT TO STOP AND PREVENT
THE JAPANESE SOLDIERS FROM MAKING WOMEN
SUFFER AGAIN. I'M REALLY FRUSTRATED THAT
AFTER 70 YEARS, THE JAPANESE GOVERNMENT
STILL HASN'T GIVEN AN APOLOGY FOR WHAT
THEY HAVE DONE. ONLY COWARDS WILL DENY
WAR CRIMES!

*COMFORT WOMEN OR MILITARY COMFORT
WOMEN IS A EUPHEMISM FOR UP TO 200,000
WOMEN, WHO SERVED IN JAPANESE MILITARY
BROTHELS DURING WORLD WAR II.

Alison Ho, 12

THE SCREAMS AND THE TERROR THAT HAPPENED
IN THIS ONE ROOM IS JUST LIKE WHAT HAPPENED
IN THOUSANDS OF ROOMS. YOUNG GIRLS WERE
STRIPPED AND LEFT NAKED IN THE ROOM. MEN,
ONE AFTER ONE CAME IN AND RAPED THESE
GIRLS. SUCH UNJUST SCENES WERE FLASHBACKS
OF GIRLS THAT WERE SEX SLAVES. AND NOW, 70
YEARS AFTER THE RAPE OF NANKING, THAT IT
IS AFFECTING LIVES…NOT EVEN AN APOLOGY
IS SAID FROM THE COWARDS — THE JAPANESE
IMPERIAL ARMY AND GOVERNMENT.

Armina Tai, 22
THE CORE OF HUMAN KIND — THE SYMBOL OF
BIRTH AND LIFE. TRUTHS WHICH WERE SHAT-
TERED ALONG WITH THE INNOCENCE OF 200,000
WOMEN, BETWEEN 1932 AND 1945, WITH ONE
TERM — "COMFORT WOMEN". NO JUSTICE CAN
COMPENSATE FOR THE HORRORS WITNESSED BY THE
VICTIMS OF HUMAN MONSTROSITY.

醒

從这个惨痛的教訓中「醒」過來！
不是「覺」，也不是「惺」，而是日本從後有
後很不敢對南京大屠殺負責及認錯，
文章給我引發了一个字。日本為什么七十七
不絕意等了一条很苦的讀者支持，我求
正南京大屠殺等等詩題。这该诚學，我亦
这个項目的北京景象及回顾一下歷史，従而引伸
而呵吧花盧溝橋与向这几个升二请航史統会
北京去，这是一个十分難得及有意思的機会，我
物品。花求时间紧迫我把这次行展，一起带川
劉美春高史織念的南京大屠殺七十周年纪念册
大学修讀漢語的女兒，回早前答应王裕佳医生及
外蒙做學術研究及交流，並順道探訪两个北京語言
今5-7青，我带同一连築系列的學生到北京情華大學及

二〇〇七青 字於北京

上的教訓：「愛人如己。」
還靠了一个猶太人——我縫明白宗教
了許多荒唐的亭奇和迫害的日子——
我做这種事並沒有良心上的不安，後來縫遇
我却时常向媽大商店的窗户擲石頭。
我父親反對我參加拿沙的反媽示威，
常常不容人民有宗教信仰自由。儒管
我的正生地波蘭在第二次世界大战以前

Prof. Albert Ng
AWAKENING

Angie Tse, 16
WHY DID THE JAPANESE GOVERNMENT ALTER THE HISTORY BOOK? TO DENY THE FORGOTTEN HOLOCAUST IS AS EVIL AS THE MASSACRE ITSELF.

Prof. Albert Ng
WHAT, WHERE, WHO, WHY, WHEN

Henry Ho
ARTIST—CHINESE CALLIGRAPHY

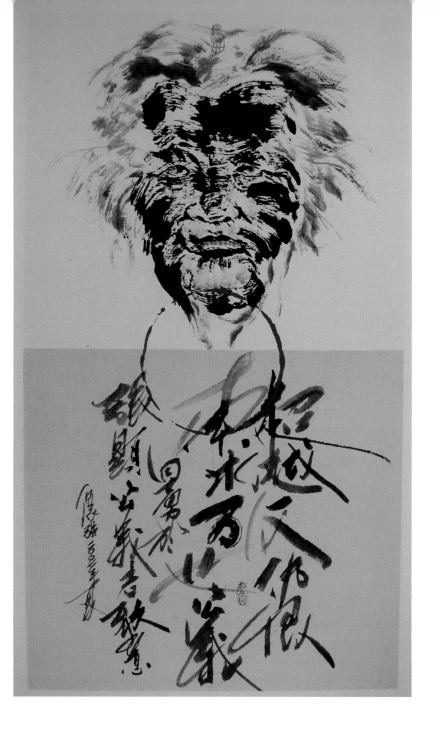

Linna Xu, 19
NANKING MASSACRE • 70TH ANNIVERSARY POSTER

Claire Yu
I FOCUSED MAINLY ON THE MASSACRES
THAT OCCURED IN NANKING AS WELL AS
THE REVIVAL OF THE TRUTH WHICH MUST
BE BROUGHT TO JUSTICE (I.E. SYMBOLIZED
BY THE HANDS).

EVERY MEDIUM OF ART OR INDIVIDUAL WORK OF ART CONTAINS AT ONE AND THE SAME TIME BOTH THE PERSONAL AND THE UNIVERSAL. IT IS BOTH A REFLECTION OF THE INDIVIDUAL ARTIST'S REACTIONS TO HIS/HER SUBJECT AS WELL AS A CONNECTION — INTENTIONAL OR NOT — SOME ASPECT OF THE WIDER HUMAN CONDITION.

IN THIS STATEMENT, I WILL FOCUS ON THE FIRST OF THESE SIDES OF THE WORK AT HAND BECAUSE I KNOW THAT IT WAS THE PRODUCT OF AN INTENSE AND PERSONAL REACTION TO THE RAPE OF NANKING. I KNOW THIS BECAUSE THE ARTIST, PO-LIN TONG KOSUTH, IS MY WIFE OF 33 YEARS, AND I KNOW HER AS WELL AS I KNOW THE TRAUMA THAT SHE EXPERIENCED IN THE CREATION OF THIS PAINTING.

EVERYTHING FOR PO-LIN IS INDIVIDUAL AND INTENSELY PERSONAL. EVERYTHING IS PUT UNDER THE MICROSCOPE AND THE MAGNIFYING GLASS OF HER ALL CONSUMING EMOTION. NO PART IS LEFT TO UNEXAMINED OR UNEXPERIENCED. THUS, FOR EACH FRAME OF BRUTAL AND SENSELESS SUFFERING DEPICTED HERE, THERE WAS AS MUCH AS IS HUMANLY POSSIBLE AN AGONY OF UNDERSTANDING AND EMPATHY.

THIS TERRIBLE INCIDENT, LIKE ANY OTHER IN THE HISTORY OF WAR, DID NOT HAVE TO HAPPEN. IT ALSO BECAME THE CATALYST FOR SOME INDIVIDUALS TO SHOW THEIR METTLE AND STAND UP IN WHATEVER WAY THEY COULD TO WHAT THEY SAW GOING ON AROUND THEM. HENCE THE REFERENCES IN THE FRAMES TO THOSE WHO DID OR COULD HAVE MADE A DIFFERENCE. THE PICTURE IS BLEAK AND DISCOURAGING AND DIFFICULT BUT NOT ENTIRELY SO. FOR THIS REASON, DURING THE PRODUCTION OF THE PAINTING, PO-LIN'S EMOTIONS RAN THE GAMUT OF SAD, ANGRY, AND OVERWHELMED BUT ALSO INSPIRED. ALL THE FRAMES WERE FILTERS FOR THESE EMOTIONS, AND A VERY FINELY GRAINED FILTER AT THAT. NOTHING PASSES THROUGH QUICKLY OR EASILY. NOTHING IS LEFT BEHIND OR TO CHANCE. EVERYTHING IS SQUEEZED AND STRAINED FOR EVERY BIT OF FEELING.

HERE PERHAPS IS A WAY TO FINISH ON THE UNIVERSAL, BUT EXACTLY HOW TO FINISH IS IN THE EYE OF THE VIEWER. THE CONTINUING LACK JUSTICE REMAINS A UNIVERSAL ISSUE BECAUSE THE PAINTING CAN BE SEEN AS NOT ONLY ABOUT THOSE WHO DIED AT NANKING BUT ALSO ABOUT THOSE WHO CONTINUE TO DIE IN IRAQ AS WELL AS THE ALL TOO UNIVERSAL ISSUE OF WHY THE CYCLE GOES ON JUST AS THE FRAMES OF THIS PAINTING ALTERNATELY PORTRAY SO MANY TERRIBLE EXAMPLES OF WHAT HAPPENED JUST AS THEY SUGGEST WHAT MIGHT HAVE BEEN. THUS, THE PERSONAL AND THE UNIVERSAL TOUCH EACH OTHER AGAIN: WHAT ONE PERSON HAS PUT INTO THE PICTURE, WHAT EACH VIEWER BRINGS AND TAKES AWAY, AND LASTLY WHAT BOTH OF THESE MIGHT CONTRIBUTE TO A DIFFERENT WORLD.

Written by Robert Kosuth, July, 2006
Artwork by po-linTong Kosuth

Canada ALPHA's
Mandate & Mission

CANADA ALPHA (ASSOCIATION FOR LEARNING AND PRESERVING THE HISTORY
OF WWII IN ASIA) IS A VOLUNTEER COMMUNITY ORGANIZATION FORMED IN
1997 WITH THREE LOCAL CHAPTERS ACROSS CANADA — BRITISH COLUMBIA,
CALGARY AND TORONTO. THE MANDATE IS TO FOSTER HUMANITY EDUCATION
AND RACIAL HARMONY WITH ITS MISSION TO PROMOTE PUBLIC AWARENESS,
LEARNING AND PRESERVATION OF THE HISTORY OF WWII IN ASIA.

Objective

We aim to preserve the truthfulness of historical records of the Second World War in Asia. Through different media, classroom teaching, and other means of communication, we spread the knowledge and the lessons learnt from the war atrocities to people around the world, which hopefully would lead to the acknowledgement of the historical facts, and acceptance of the responsibilities of the war by Japan. The eventual objective is to pursue justice for the victims of the war, remove hatred and suspicion, resulting in peace and harmony among people.

Declaration

Japan, as a leading economy in the Asian Pacific area, could have a beneficial influence over the peoples of Asia if she could have a relationship of mutual respect and lasting peace with her neighboring countries. Unfortunately, during the Second World War, the Japanese military regime invaded Asian countries and raided Pearl Harbor while German Nazis overran Europe. This brought about profound tragedies and brutal war crimes so numerous as to take a long time to relate.

With the War behind us for over 50 years, Germany had long admitted to committing atrocities and made compensations for her victims. Japan, on the other hand, has so far dodged the issues of formal apology and compensation for her war crimes. Instead, in recent years, some influential Japanese politicians tried to whitewash the invasion as the protection of Asia from Western imperialism, and the Education Ministry altered history textbooks to cover up the truth. Such shortsighted measures will only be an insult to Asian nations and arouse racial hostilities and hatred.

In line with Canada's national policy of multiculturalism and racial harmony, we want to maintain harmonious relations with the ethnic Japanese community. But we deplore the unrelenting Japanese militarism.

To bring justice to the sufferings of the Asian people during WWII, Japan must formally admit her mistakes, sincerely apologize for her crimes and offer reasonable compensation for damages incurred. Only then will the future generations come to see the militarist warmongers for what they were, and not repeat their mistakes. Only then will truth be restored to history.

The way to peace is to respect and learn from history. This is the goal of our association.

INCORPORATION OF ASIAN WWII HISTORY INTO THE B.C. GRADE 11–12 CURRICULUM

Iris Chang's book was a major reference to the teachers' guide on "Human Rights in the Asia Pacific 1931-1945: Social responsibility and Global Citizenship", jointly published by the BC Ministry of Education and BC ALPHA in 2001. This guide is first of its kind in the world featuring human rights violations during WW II in Asia for high school students.

A RESOURCE GUIDE FOR TEACHERS TO SUPPORT ASPECTS OF SENIOR SOCIAL STUDIES CURRICULUM

Human Rights in the Asia Pacific 1931-1945

SOCIAL RESPONSIBILITY AND GLOBAL CITIZENSHIP

BRITISH COLUMBIA
Ministry of Education

B.C. Association for Learning & Preserving the History of WW II in Asia

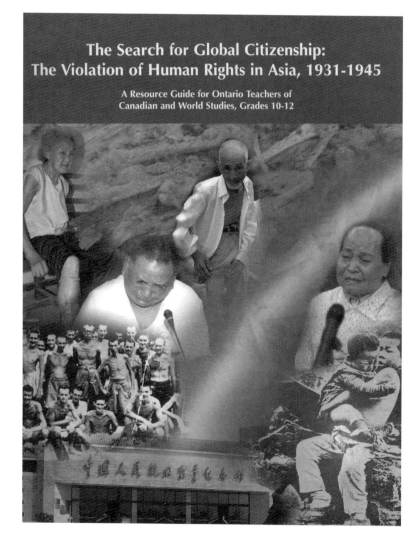

The Search for Global Citizenship:
The Violation of Human Rights in Asia, 1931-1945

A Resource Guide for Ontario Teachers of
Canadian and World Studies, Grades 10-12

DEVELOPMENT OF THE FIRST ON-TARIO TEACHERS' RESOURCE GUIDE ON ASIAN WWII HISTORY

To assist and support teachers to teach this history, Toronto ALPHA formed a working group with educators and study tour participants to write and compile a comprehensive resource guide entitled, The Search for Global Citizenship: The Violation of Human Rights in Asia, 1931-1945 (A Resource Guide for Ontario Teachers of Canadian and World Studies, Grades 10-12). This document, which is available online (www.asia-wwii.org), provides teachers with information about historical events and the related human rights issues, as well as suggested lessons, teaching expectations, easy-to-use resource materials, and reference lists. ◆

The Peace & Reconciliation Study Tour

BACKGROUND

To support the Social Studies Curriculum, the BC Ministry of Education published the Social Studies teachers' guide Human Rights in the Asia Pacific 1931-1945: Social Responsibility and Global Citizenship in 2001. The French version of the resource is also available for French immersion schools. It is to support the pre-scribed learning outcomes for Social Studies Grade 11, History 12 and Law 12. Its objective is to develop students' appreciation of Canada as part of a much larger humanity and their sense of global fraternity and responsibility. This is an excel-lent class tool for peace and justice education and for fighting against racism. It is the world's first teachers' guide using humanity issues in the history of the Asia-Pacific War to teach human rights and global citizenship.

As a partner in the development of the B.C. learning resource, ALPHA has taken the initiative to offer continual support to teachers in the effective and creative use of this education tool. We can help arrange speakers, survivors and eyewit-nesses for classes, and make available on loan to teachers reference and video materials and also traveling exhibits on humanity issues of this tragic history. In line with this spirit, the annual Peace & Reconciliation Study Tour has been conducted since 2004.

SHANGHAI DAILY REPORTS ON THE PEACE & RECON-
CILIATION STUDY TOUR WHICH PROVIDES FIRSTHAND
INFORMATION ON THE ASIAN HOLOCAUST.

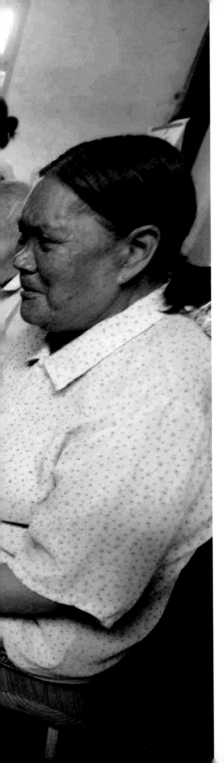

OBJECTIVE

To enhance teachers' knowledge and understanding of the cultural and historical background of China during the Asia-Pacific War.

To facilitate teachers' personal brush with this chapter of history through meeting survivors, visiting museums and historical sites.

To facilitate teachers' reflection on the legacy of the Asia-Pacific War and how it impacts on peace through meeting with historians and teachers in China as well as scholars and lawyers supporting survivors' quest for justice.

To facilitate teachers' sharing of their experience in the teaching of social responsibility and global citizenship, including developing ideas and teaching methods in using the learning resources "Human Rights in the Asia Pacific 1931-1945: Social Responsibility and Global Citizenship"

KEY CITIES VISITED
- Shanghai
- Nanjing
- Harbin
- Beijing (departure city)
- Yiwu

[LEFT] DR. LAU MING JARM OF TORONTO ALPHA EXAMINES THE FESTERING WOUND OF AN ANTHRAX VICTIM, MADAM WANG JUHUA

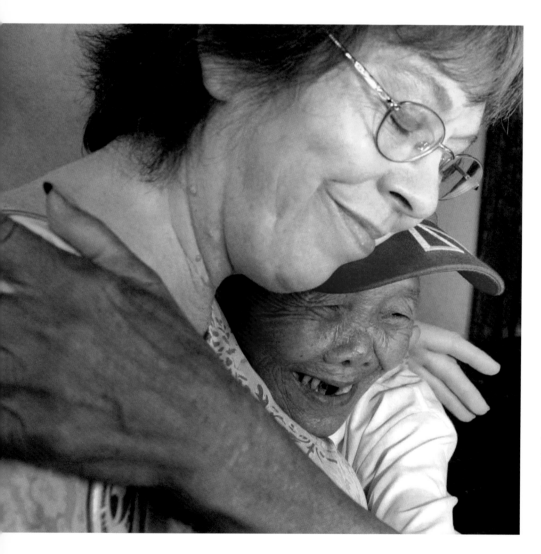

A HEART-TOUCHING MOMENT: CAREL MCDONALD, A BRITISH COLUMBIAN TEACHER EMBRACING MADAM XU, A GERM WARFARE SURVIVOR.

TOUR PERIOD ITINERARY 2007

- June 30 – July 14, 2007 including acclimatization from June 30 to July 37
- Mandatory sessions start on evening of July 3 (Tuesday): All participants are required to check-in at the arranged hotel in Shanghai and assemble for orientation at 6:00 p.m.
- Last day of tour (July 16, Monday): The Study Tour will be considered dispersed after the Concluding Session to be ended at noon.
- The arrival and departure dates of the Tour need to be strictly observed. For participants who may like to self arrange a tour of China or other countries before and after the Study Tour, they need to work around these dates.
- Please note that attendance at all sessions from July 3 – 14 is mandatory unless otherwise specified.

OUTLINE OF ACTIVITIES

- Meeting survivors of military sexual slavery (the so-called "comfort women"), forced labour, chemical & biological warfare and Nanking Massacre
- Meeting historians and researchers on humanity issues of the Asia-Pacific War
- Sharing with teachers on the education of this chapter of history.
- Meeting lawyers and scholars supporting the redress of victims.
- Visiting museums and historical sites related to humanity issues of the Asia-Pacific War.
- Reflection and sharing sessions.
- Sightseeing and to know more about the people and culture of China.

A COMFORT WOMAN SHARES
HER TRAGIC STORY WITH THE
STUDY TOUR PARTICIPANTS.

COSTS

- ALPHA is responsible for all group travel, accommodation (Two persons per room) and meal expenses during the period of the Study Tour.
- Teachers are responsible for their own return international airfare from Canada to China, visitor visa's fee, international airport taxes as well as their personal medical and accident insurance covering the period of the Study Tour. This is a mandatory requirement and the insured value is a personal   decision of the participants.
- Teachers are responsible for their own personal expenses and substitution costs, if any.

DUTIES

After the study tour, selected teachers are expected to:

- Prepare and make a presentation at the report-back sessions organized by ALPHA.
- Integrate the teachers' guide "Human Rights in the Asia Pacific 1931–1945: Social Responsibility and Global Citizenship" into the courses for which it was designed.
- Provide feedback and make recommendation to ALPHA for better use of this learning resource by other teachers.
- Make individual or group presentations at teachers' conferences to report-back on the tour and to share resources and experience in the teaching of this chapter of history. ◆

南京大屠殺・七十周年
Nanking Massacre • 70th Anniversary

Study Tour 2007
Teachers' Journals

STUDY TOUR 2007

July 1, 2007
Arriving in Shanghai

July 2, 2007
Shanghai — Acclimatization

DAVID YATES

It's hard to get used to the idea that I'm finally in China. This was a place that only existed on a map until now.

The heat and humidity was the first thing to hit us as we disembarked from the aircraft. It wasn't an oppressive heat but it did serve to remind us that we're in sub-tropical climate.

In the quick maglev ride through the Shanghai suburbs one can see the new modern China contrasted with the old. Tall, modern high rise apartments tower over old crumbling clay row houses. At first glance some of them look to be uninhabited but then the clothesline in the back alley indicates that people live there.

I'm amazed at how westernized Shanghai is. A lot of the advertisements display western models and the writing

JULIE PLUNKETT

Today was our first official day in Shanghai!! Our tour guide, Michael, shared with us lots of information about the city. It is an incredibly modern city and the architecture is phenomenal; it is highly creative and each design appears to have a specific meaning or purpose.

In the morning, we visited Dr. Sun Yat-Sen's house. I did not know very much about him and was impressed by his many accomplishments. He was an incredible man that orchestrated the first republic in China. His passion for the Chinese people inspired many changes in China and he is much beloved and respected by everyone that I met in China. This man's faith in humanity and his dedication to helping others truly highlighted to me the importance of providing a voice to the silent victims of the Rape of Nanking.

After lunch, we visited the Shanghai Museum. It is difficult to express in words the rich and intricate collection of art and artefacts that depicts the intricate history of the Chinese people.

My initial impressions of Shanghai are wonderful. I find it to be a vibrant city full of innovation, history and kindness towards all of us visiting from Canada. I look forward to learning more about China and embarking on the study component of this tour.

July 3, 2007
Shanghai and Wu Zhen

MICHAEL DOYLE

Wu Zhen, our destination for our out-of-town day trip did not disappoint. It is a city of bridges — 40 now remain of the original 120 — Fu Lan Chiao being its oldest. Wu Zhen also is the home of 200 famous Chinese scholars.

A washroom break on the way to Wu Zhen proved to be interesting as some of us watered the flowers, and others squatted for the first time. The drive there was not without its sights — pigs, paddies, and rural population.

After a nice lunch we all enjoyed an enchanting boat ride along the canal in the old city at Wu Zhen. The old buildings still being lived in gave us all a glimpse of Chinese life from long ago — a plethora of opportunity for our cameras.

We were given some free time to roam through the narrow alleys — 10 feet wide in places — where I for one sweated heavily. Some shopped, some shopped and fanned, and some watched the traditional Shadow Play.

The way home gave us a taste of Shanghai traffic before we were to taste our first authentic Chinese dim sum. We were then whisked away — banana and chocolate ice cream still on our lips and headed over to the Arts Centre to watch ERA — the acrobatic show. This was an amazing spectacle. Filled with adrenaline, music, energy and grace, those of us who managed to fight off the jet lag were treated to a lively evening.

July 4, 2007
Shanghai Normal University

ZOE MUGFORD

We awoke to a rainy day in Shanghai. Having shed the worst of the jet lag, we were ready to begin our programme; the reason we have travelled all this way. We really started with a resounding bang.

We arrived at the campus of Shanghai Normal University before 9am. The campus was quite beautiful, soggy, but charming.

Professor Su entered the room, and our programme began. He proceeded to give us an overview of the Opium Wars, and the occupation of Shanghai by western powers. The lecture had particular resonance, because we had already visited some of those former concessions, and seen the diversity and influence in the architecture and economy of those areas.

The afternoon had a different tone entirely. It almost seemed like the climax of the trip on the first day of the programme. That — of course — was the introduction of Madam Lin Ya-Jin. She looked fragile and frail walking next to the two young women helping her. She wore a simple headscarf, shirt and skirt, practical and subdued. She had a dignity and strength about her that belied her tiny frame, a strong and erect posture held by her tiny spine. Once seated, she began to tell us her story. Through our two translators, we learned how the Japanese used and abused her, how her husband betrayed her, how her mother fought to cure her, and how she fought, and persevered, and survived. She cried at times, and we all cried with her, internally for some and externally for others. She cried when she spoke of the Japanese beating her, saying that she was so small, and should not be so strong and fight so hard. She cried again when she spoke of the husband who left her, and whom she still loved.

She was asked if she still harbours resentment toward the Japanese of today. I cringed a little hearing the question; as a Japanese Canadian I was wary to know. She grew up in a village and did not have much of a formal education. I had no need to fear, her answer was "no". She said she has a great awareness of truth, and of right and wrong, and she could see that the Japanese of today were not to blame. If only we too could all be so forgiving and apply that lesson to our own lives. She also said she believes victory is on her side. I hope she is able to see this in her lifetime. I know we will all endeavour to see it in ours.

One of the most poignant moments of a momentous day was when Maureen presented her gift to Madam Lin. It was a maple leaf quilt that she had taken the time to make herself. She made a beautiful speech, and draped it around Madam Lin's shoulder. I think we all felt as though we were wrapping around her too. It was a tremendous moment, one that I will never forget.

No doubt, we were all somewhere lost in our thoughts, inspired by the strength and the courage and the story of survivor Lin Ya-jin.

TEACHERS MEETING WITH HISTORIANS AT THE NANJING NORMAL UNIVERSITY

July 5, 2007
Shanghai — "Comfort Women" Research Institute

TEACHERS REACT EMOTIONALLY
TO TESTIMONIES.

MARY MURTHA

We once again met Madam Lin, this time at the opening of the "Comfort Women" Archives. These archives are the result of more than thirty years of research by Professor Su and many others. For the occasion, Madam Lin was joined by two other former Comfort Women: one was a tenacious, energetic woman who had assisted the Chinese army, and because of this was not just raped by the Japanese but tortured as well, and one was a woman who conceived a baby as a result of the repeated rape by Japanese soldiers. The latter was accompanied by her son.

I'm still not sure what to think about the last two days; so many emotions are fighting to get to the front of my mind, it will take some time to process them all. I'm greatly conflicted by the history teacher side of me, which recognizes the immeasurable value of this first-person testimony, and the more emotional, human side which worries that perhaps we are somehow exploiting these women. They are here to tell their stories of being violated by foreigners for selfish purposes — are we doing something similar? Of course, there is a monumental difference between the violence that was inflicted on these women without their consent, and their willing assistance of our pursuit of truth and historical knowledge. Yet somehow I still wondered if we were using these women — parading them and their suffering before us and the camera crews, so that we can feel better about ourselves as Western tourists and students of history, feel that we truly "get" their suffering, before we retreat back into the bus, into our trivial chatter about what to have for dinner and what to see in Shanghai that night. And these women are left alone with their scars, their pain and their unimaginable emotional trauma.

I'm not discounting how meaningful it has been for me (and, I imagine, all of us) to hear Madam Lin, and the other women's stories. I know that I will always carry with me the faraway look in her dark eyes, the sound of her rough sobs as she told us her story of kidnap, rape, beatings, abandonment and loneliness. But I will also feel like this is not enough. No matter what I do with this information, this experience is not enough. It won't erase the guilt I felt at watching a frail, elderly woman who has experienced abuse after abuse in her life, sob in front of a room full of people while those physically closest to her chose not to put their arms around her for comfort, but rather to jockey for position for the best photograph…

The second half of the day was spent touring a former comfort house. It's amazing how a place with such quiet elegance — the tall, intricate metal doors; the wide, open-air stone courtyard — could have been the site of such unutterable horror. To see the hallways where the soldiers would have lined up, pushing and joking with each other, as if they were lining up to get into a bar, and the rooms where the women would have fought, cried, screamed and eventually acquiesced, is chilling.

As a history teacher, I am familiar with instances of genocide around the world, and I know the unspeakable horrors of which the human heart is capable. However, there is something about the cold organization, the detached bureaucracy, of this system, of this place, that makes it somehow especially evil.

After we had spent about an hour exploring the two floors of the area, Julie M., Bob and I found ourselves locked inside the house. The rest of the group had — sensibly — retreated into the air-conditioning of the bus, and the managers of the site assumed everyone was gone, so they padlocked the door. It only took us a few minutes to find someone with a key to let us out, but the anxiety it caused made me think about the dozens of women who couldn't leave this place until they were irrevocably damaged, or — more likely — dead. What a place, what a way, to leave this world. What a final impression of humanity. I try to imagine it, but I guess our struggle and our salvation is that those who have never experienced such evil, will never know how it feels.

After debriefing this difficult, emotional day in our (very cathartic) first Group Meeting, I went back to my hotel room and fell asleep easily — I guess, the way only a Western tourist, who tomorrow is moving on from this place, can.

A STATUE OF JOHN RABE.

July 7, 2007
Nanjing
The John Rabe Museum

ANGELA WAN

Today on our second day in Nanjing we visited the John Rabe Museum based in the original office buildings of Siemens where Rabe once worked. I am drawn to this simple building which reminded me of houses that are seen in children's storybooks. It is overwhelming for me that at one time, many regarded this place as a safe haven and indeed many lives were spared here. This small room was a perfect setting for our continuing journey into the study of the Nanking Massacre. After a brief introduction to Rabe's background we ventured into the museum where we walked through many images, testimonials and artefacts of the period. It was very clear to me that the two main historical figures of this WWII story, John Rabe and Minnie Vautrin, were well-loved and respected by the people of Nanjing. By saving ten of thousands of lives, they were indeed the 'Buddha' and 'Goddess' of Nanjing.

At this part of the journey, one main theme resonated in my mind — the unbelievable ability of an individual to put the needs of others ahead of himself/herself. How were individuals like John Rabe and Minnie Vautrin able to see past the dangers around them? How were they able to set aside the privileges available to them and attend to the needs of the Chinese people who in many aspects were very different from themselves? In such times of crisis when many are at moral crossroads, where does one find the strength to do what is right?

This study tour has been a challenge to my body, mind, and soul. The history that I have learned about my people has questioned my faith in humanity but the survivors give me hope and inspiration. In their voices I hear strength and perseverance and in their eyes I see hope and resilience. This has been an incredible experience, one that I look forward to sharing with my friends, family, and future generations.

A PLAQUE AT THE JOHN RABE MUSEUM, INDI-CATING WHERE JOHN RABE LIVED.

July 8, 2007
Nanjing

JULIE MCCALLUM

The first stop was the Bei Jie Gou Monument — one of 13 memorials built in the 1950s to commemorate the lives lost. The next stop was on a cliff overlooking the river. Some brave souls faced the waves of water cascading down the stairs leading to the cliff where an estimated 57,000 unarmed Chinese men were gunned down. Inconceivable. That's the amount of people at a sold out Blue Jays game at the Dome. It makes me think — how can this be? I am filled with disbelief and sadness for the lives lost and the lives affected, but also because young soldiers were responsible for this. What (other than orders) could make an individual feel so superior to another? I have questions and yet there are no answers.

Once we reached the city gate called Jiangdong — symbolism took on a whole new meaning. This memorial was simple, but left lasting impressions. The five rings of the memorial (representing the 5 zeroes in the 300,000 Chinese murdered in 6 weeks) and the bell (representing peace) stood out amongst the modern day war zone.

We headed back to the site from yesterday (Rabe house) where we met with Duan Yue Ping, former Director of the Nanjing Museum. I found her to be a very kind woman. As she spoke, Ning Ping listened and translated for us into English. Watching this process, it got my mind to wondering, how does Ning Ping feel about all of this? In most instances she retells horrific stories and becomes the voice of another person. This seems to me quite glorious and also daunting. I think for myself — having her speak is wonderful — because it is the voice of a friend, but I worry about her. Overall, Ms. Duan was very informative filling in some gaps of info. Some was a recap of information (stats of killings and rapes that took place), but everything is still unbelievable no matter how many times I hear it. Again, how can this be?

ALPHA ON TOUR OF UNIT 731 MUSEUM, HARBIN, CHINA

July 10, 2007
Harbin — Unit 731

JENNIFER GEE

I am still processing the horror or Unit 731. It has made an impact on me like nothing else that I have experienced in my life. It seems to be the kind of thing that my mind processes in small bits, as though the immensity of the grief is too overwhelming for my brain to deal with all at once.

I think one of the most horrifying aspects of it is the fact that the building looks so "normal", like any number of other factories or institutions that you could find almost anywhere in the world. There is something so disquieting about evil looking so normal.

The pictures that we've seen of the doctors and the soldiers who committed barbaric acts are likewise very "normal" looking. I can see family members, neighbours, teachers and other people that I know in the faces of those doctors and soldiers. And then I hear the stories of the things that happened at Unit 731, the things that doctors did in the name of following. I think Gandhi was right by saying that 'science without humanity can destroy us'. People can use anything (science, religion, politics, language etc) for their own selfish and sadistic purposes if they are so inclined. But it is so sad. Why inclines someone to that? What are the factors that contribute to acts of depravity being seen as preferable to compassion? I need to search my soul for the answers to that…

Unit 731 has a heavy silence around it. I think it's the silence of grief. I feel the same way at many funerals and some cemeteries. It's sad to think that the faces of uncaring doctors and scientists are the last faces that innocent victims looked on before they died. In a way, I am glad that the names of the majority of victims are not known — I know it sounds weird to say. At first I was outraged because people should be

able to properly pay their respects. On the other hand, this way the victims can be remembered for their lives and not for their undoubtedly excruciating deaths. Their names will not be associated with such dehumanizing cruelty. I hope they're able to have some level of dignity because of this. It's ironic: the Japanese called these victims "logs" in an effort to dehumanize them. However, because of that we don't know the victims' names and we do know the names of the scientists and doctors. The doctors and scientists should have their names associated with what they did; the dehumanization belongs to the perpetrators not the victims.

I don't know how my mind will incorporate the knowledge of Unit 731 into my life. I know that it will be there and that it will inform my understanding of faith and morality and humanity. But how exactly it will manifest I have yet to see. It is so much to digest and

I'm not sure I will ever be able to make sense of it. I do know that I am exceedingly grateful for having been able to walk through the site. In a way, the darkness of that place helped me be so much more grateful for the light that I see in my own life. Unit 731 will stay with me for quite some time.

TEACHERS HAVE ESTABLISHED A SPECIAL RAPPORT WITH ELDER GENG ZHUN WHO WAS ABDUCTED TO WORK IN HANAOKA OF JAPAN AND LATER LED THE UPRISING OF THE FORCED LABOURERS.

July 11, 2007
Harbin

SIMONE SCOTT

I went to the "Heart of Darkness" today. The dank, cavernous building which was the death factory of Unit 731 resembles a tomb. The feeling of tortured spirits and unending despair weighed heavily on me. I felt that I was staring into the abyss of human depravity.

Inside I looked for something redemptive, but found nothing. The most seemingly benign artefacts all had a darker purpose. While wandering through I thought about the victims. What did they think? What efforts did they make to survive? Were they able to show life-affirming kindness to each other in the face of soul-destroying conditions?

As I wandered around, I noticed that the building was falling into disrepair. How does one preserve a monument to evil? Should it be knocked to the ground, restored, or left to the vagaries of nature? From the dilapidated state of this place, it seems that the Chinese are also grappling with this idea.

On this trip we have been plagued by spectres of the very worst of the human condition. Only the callous can say, "This has nothing to do with me. I was not involved. These are not my people." One hears that all too often, about what people feel they are and are not responsible for. People use these arguments for not doing what is right or just. It never occurs to them that they are living on the cumulative pain of others. They want to start the clock of social justice only after they have arrived. But one is born into history. One isn't born into a void.

As I was leaving the grounds I encountered a Japanese film crew. They were there to uncover the secrets of Unit 731 that the Japanese government has long kept from its people. It was led by a medical doctor who, having been trained by some of the perpetrators of human experiments, suspected that their methods crossed the bounds of medical ethics. After years of research, the trail led him to Harbin. And so we met in a field beside an abandoned railway, not speaking each others' language, yet united in our desire for full disclosure, greater understanding, and healing.

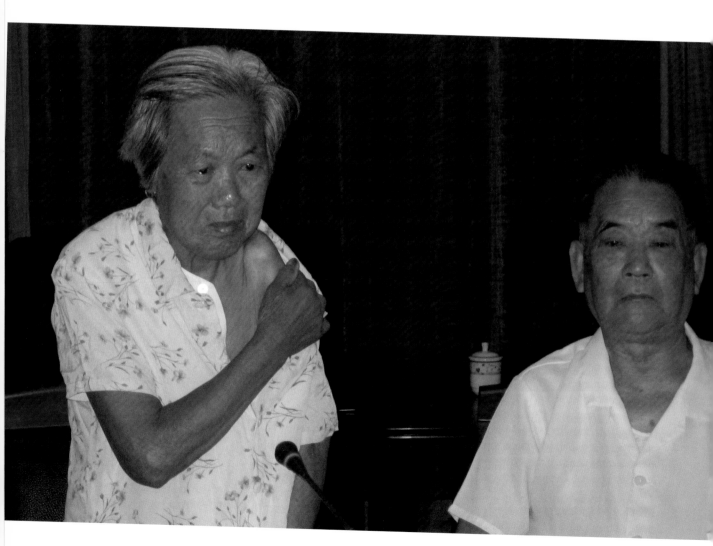

A FORMER COMFORT WOMAN GIVES TESTIMONY IN NANJING, CHINA.

July 14, 2007
Aftermath

ELLEN FRANCIS

I write this on the plane — just two hours out of Beijing- unable to fully comprehend the journey I've just experienced but also fully cognizant of a depth- which cannot be realized at the moment. The last few days — since July 11 particularly have had a profound effect on me-and I guess the theme of these remarks would have to be" aftermath". The story of the last victim — forced labourer resonates within me still, particularly the strength which he displayed to seek redress- not just for himself but for his children.

In the face of helplessness, look at what strong minded individuals can do when they believe in something so important such as social justice. The message of the consequences of human atrocities for the Chinese victims is an important lesson for our students and I believe that in our post modern world, the dignity and worth of the individual becomes increasingly important. The "aftermath" so far, for me, of this trip is the reminder that discrimination takes root in small beginnings and we should carefully reflect upon our treatment of others — to think about the significance of our actions. This might be the starting point — the aftermath when I step off the plane. ◆

Joanna Fu, 15
THE PAIN THAT EACH WOMAN FELT PIERCED THROUGH THEIR HEART AND
MIND LIKE A NEVER-ENDING CHAIN OF MEMORY. THE BLOOD THAT WAS LOST
SHALL NEVER BE FORGOTTEN IN THE MINDS OF TODAY.

Our Forever Iris...
In commemorating the Forgotten Unforgettable

Message from the Chair and Vice Chair of Toronto and Canada ALPHA

2005 marked the 60th Anniversary of the end of World War II.

When we were organizing the first fund-raising dinner for Toronto ALPHA, we gave the title 'The Ray of Hope — 60 years later' for the event. The title originated from our sentiment that in 1997, on the 60th Anniversary of the Rape of Nanking, Iris Chang, with her book on the subject, actually gave us a ray of hope, amid all darkness and hopelessness, that this dark chapter of history would finally start to unearth.

With her premature and untimely death, all of us felt a great sense of loss and a determination that Iris' legacy has to continue. We remembered that after reading the book excerpt and review on Iris's book in a November 1997 issue of Newsweek, we started to see a faint light that this horrible war crime would not be forever concealed. We invited Iris to come to Canada to help promote her book during the 60th Anniversary of the Rape of Nanking. Her book attracted major media attention in Vancouver and Toronto, and the rest, as the saying goes, is history. The volunteers of ALPHA, in both Vancouver and Toronto, were greatly inspired by Iris and her 7 to 8 days of stay in Canada were among the most memorable times in the lives of many volunteers.

It was this state of mind and our fond memory of Iris that we started to plan something for 2007 — the 70th Anniversary of the Nanking Massacre. A film portraying Iris's life and spirit, linked with the historic event, was conceived. In the ensuing winter and spring, we were talking to a lot of people who were experienced in the film-making business. We came across Anne and Bill, who also happened to be thinking about doing similar project after they read Iris' book. We were quite excited about the partnership with them being the co-directors and producer. In exchanging our knowledge and passion, we went through many hurdles and shared many experiences. We are confident that the film will earn years of solid and stellar reputation in documentary film-making in Canada.

The next challenges were to convince the parents of Iris to cooperate with us, and to raise necessary financial resources to make the film, which could be quite substantial. We overcame both hurdles in our trip to California in mid-2006, visiting Iris's parents and talking to the Board of the Avery-Tsui Founda-

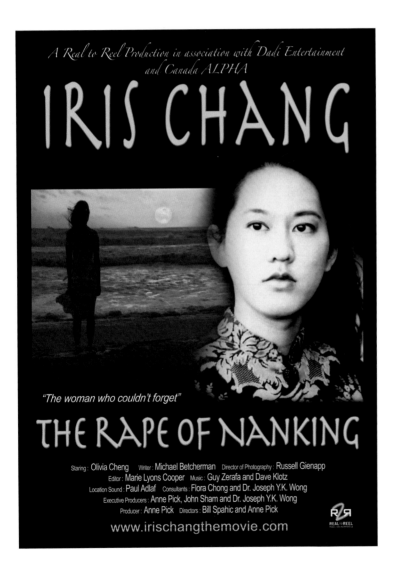

The last two years has been an emotional and rewarding journey in our lives. It also marked a significant milestone along our path towards truth and righteousness, peace and reconciliation.

tion. The rest of the required funds was raised in Toronto. Altogether, over 3000 individual donors turned this dream into a reality.

The film ' Iris Chang ' far exceeds our best expectations, thanks to Anne and Bill and their team. We are so touched and inspired that we hope 'Iris Chang 'would also be remembered as one of the most inspiring films of all time, and that the passion behind the film would ignite the fire in each of our hearts.

There are so many people we want to thank for their invaluable contribution in the making of this film. First of all, we want to thank the parents of Iris, Ying-Ying and Shau-Jin, for their trust in us and sharing the story of their daughter and their families with us. We want to thank Olivia Cheng and Yo-Yo Sham, two young and very talented women, for helping making the film, and writing and composing the theme song. Our other Co-Execu-

tive Producer and a good friend, John Sham, contributed a lot of resources and connections in Asia. There are literally thousands of people in Toronto who have contributed whatever they could to help preserve this history and pursue justice for the victims. We want to thank particularly the generous donations from Ellen Pun, Ida Li and Glenn Chan, Lena Au-Yeung, Philip Chong, Irene and Frank Chau, Charles Chan, and many others too numerous to enlist here.

The people to whom we owe the most are the board members of the Avery-Tsui Foundation. Without their encouragement and generosity, this film would simply be impossible.

The last two years has been an emotional and rewarding journey in our lives. It also marked a significant milestone along our path towards truth and righteousness, peace and reconciliation. While we greet our chal-

lenges and count our blessings, we also treasure every moment we had in actualizing this amazing dream.

DR. JOSEPH Y. K. WONG, C.M.
CO-EXECUTIVE PRODUCER OF 'IRIS CHANG'
CHAIR, TORONTO ALPHA
CO-FOUNDER, CANADA ALPHA

FLORA CHONG
PROJECT COORDINATOR OF 'IRIS CHANG'
VICE-CHAIR, TORONTO AND CANADA ALPHA

Olivia Cheng
LEADING ACTRESS PLAYING THE

ROLE OF IRIS CHANG

When I first saw Iris Chang on the cover of Readers' Digest a decade ago, I never could've imagined then that I'd one day travel around the world to play her in a movie. The entire experience has been an eye opening journey and an incredibly humbling honor. Although I'll never have the chance to meet Iris in person, her spirit obviously lives on as her legacy continues to unite people from all walks of life in a common cause. What struck me the most about some of the words Iris left behind is her belief in "The Power of One". What if we all lived by that saying and found ways to move forward in spite of the fears and doubts that challenge us along the way? Imagine what your 'Power of One' can do for the world and go do it. Or as some might say, go Iris Chang it.

Anne Pick
FILM PRODUCER AND CO-DIRECTOR

Iris and her book, The Rape of Nanking, together have been like a pebble in the water, creating many ripples of knowledge and understanding. It has united so many of us to carry on her quest: to honour the victims of the Nanking massacre, to tell the world the truth about what happened in that dark time beginning in December 1937, to give voice to the remaining survivors and push for an uncompromising apology and reparations from Japan. The survivors shared their stories with Iris and subsequently with us, despite the heartache, to better inform the world about what happened in Nanking, and to remind us that war brings nothing but pain. We cried with them. Longevity inevitably brings with it wisdom and they all had a message of peace and reconciliation. So many amazing things happened during the production of this film it is difficult to even begin but it can honestly be said that it was a life changing experience for us all. Iris and the survivors touched our hearts and souls. It has been a privilege to bring Iris and the story of Nanking, to the screen for us all.

Bill Spahic
FILM CO-DIRECTOR

Right from the start we wanted to make a docu-drama via Iris' character because we felt it would help the audience understand that this was not just statistics and historical dates but rather it was personal and painful experience for hundreds of thousands who died and those who survived and those who are still alive today. This is the feeling we got from reading Iris' book. Because Iris was no longer with us we decided to use archival footage of her and augment with our wonderful actress Olivia Cheng to get below the surface of this holocaust-as Iris herself experienced it.

Everyone helped us wherever we turned, but the most helpful was Iris herself. She was our guiding light. There are many parallels between her writing her book and our making the film. Many times I felt that Iris was looking after us. The most obvious example of this is the 4 VHS tapes (her filming survivors). She left a copy of the tapes behind in Nanjing with Prof Yang in '95 who gave us the tapes in Dec 2006 when we first filmed there. The original tapes no longer exist. Those copies she left behind for us proved a gold mine visually but more importantly it gave us a real first hand understanding of how Iris felt hearing the survivors' stories. It was as if she were saying here, this is what I heard…it was easy to imagine how she felt.

Shau-Jin & Ying-Ying Chang
PARENTS OF IRIS CHANG

As a child, Iris always enjoyed talking to us especially around the dinner table. Our conversation frequently touched our family history. Sino-Japanese war and the Rape of Nanking were among the stories that we told her. Shau-Jin's dad was the mayor of Taicang, a port city adjacent to Shanghai where Japan invading force landed. He and his city workers helped the defending army to hold the city for three months. At Nanjing, Ying-Ying's mom and her sister nearly missed the last boat to leave Nanjing. To Iris, it was a miracle that all of her grand parents survived. When Iris saw an exhibition on Nanking Massacre at Cupertino, CA in 1994, she decided that she had to write a book on the Rape of Nanking. These dinner table stories of her childhood formed the seed of her decision. Throughout the writing of her book, we had given her encouragement as well as her physical and emotional support as much as we could. It was on the 60th anniversary of The Rape of Nanking that Iris published her famous book. Now, the 70th anniversary of The Rape of Nanking is coming. We are happy to see that the film " Iris Chang — The Rape of Nanking" by Anne Pick, Bill Spahic, and Joseph Y. K. Wong will be ready for the occasion. We hope that this film will accomplish as a film what Iris' The Rape of Nanking did as a book. We're always behind Iris for fighting the justice and truth. We hope one day the truth will prevail and the tragedy such as the Rape of Nanking will never happen in the world!

Yo-Yo Sham
PRODUCTION ASSISTANT, TRANSLATOR, THEME SONG WRITER, SINGER

When I decided to join this film, I was looking for something that would get me closer to the 'reality' I keep hearing about. I was only aware of my unawareness of things we ought to know.

While I met people I could never have met otherwise, asked questions I never thought to ask, and shared memories that wouldn't have been shared with me if not for this film, my heart cried more than it ever did. Reality is — many had experienced the unimaginable, and too many of us are unaware.

If not for this film, I wouldn't have gone so far to get to know Iris. As we walked the paths she walked in Nanjing, I realized that I was not only inspired, I began to feel a bond with her — someone I've never met and could never meet. I submerged myself into the project, partly in attempt to know more about her, and contributed in every way I

know of. In return I've gained more than I had hoped for; I'm lucky and am very grateful.

If not for Olivia, I wouldn't begin to imagine myself in the soundtrack. If not for Anne and Bill, I wouldn't be writing here and would have nothing to write about. If not for Iris, this film wouldn't be. I sincerely hope this film will touch someone's heart; the way making it touched mine.

THE CREW FILING THE DOCUDRAMA IN
NANKING, CHINA — THE CITY WHERE THE
ORIGINAL MASSACRE OCCURED.

NI CUI-PING, A SURVIVIOR OF THE NANKING MASSACRE, GETS EMOTIONAL DURING FILMING.

A BEHIND THE SCENES LOOK AT THE CREW, RIDING THE BUS TO THE SET AND TAKING A LOOK AT A CUT OF THE FILM.

[LEFT] FOORPRINTS OF SURVIVORS INSIDE THE
NANKING MASSACRE VICTIMS MEMORIAL HALL.
[RIGHT] INTERVIEWING JAPANESE ACTIVIST SAYOKO
AT THE 69TH ANNIVERSARY CEREMONY INSIDE THE
MEMORIAL HALL.

THE FILM CREW IN CHINA.

MEDIA RELEASE FOR THE FILM IN NANJING AND HONG KONG. **[TOP LEFT]** OLIVIA CHENG AND 'LITTLE IRIS'. **[TOP RIGHT]** SHAU-JIN AND YING-YING CHANG, THE PARENTS OF IRIS CHANG SPEAK ABOUT THE FILM. **[LEFT]** JOHN SHUM, JOSEPH Y.K. WONG, AND FLORA CHONG OF ALPHA CANADA.

FILM PROMOTION CONFERENCE IN HONG KONG.

"Iris Chang—the Rape of Nanking" Theme Song

Lyrics OLIVIA CHENG/YO-YO SHAM

A1

Just a little child
they took it all away
Your blood, your life
Your trust, your faith
You died reborn in pain

Red as the river,
looming large the gate
Darkness in your heart,
drowning in their hate

I'll dedicate my life to get
your stories told

CHORUS

I'll give voice to the voiceless
Silenced for too long
Crying out for justice
Trust me with your pain
I'll take it as my own
I'll fight to get the truth heard
My weapon is my word

A2

One more time, remember
The horror and the pain
They raped you of your pride
robbed of your dignity

Speak of how they stole your peace
screaming for them to cease

CHORUS
I'll give voice to the voiceless
Silenced for too long
Crying out for justice
Trust me with your pain
I'll take it as my own
I'll fight to get the truth heard
My weapon is my word

BRIDGE
It's done. The pages filled
With blood and tears
Not in vain
The world will finally hear

CHORUS
I gave voice to the voiceless
Now I'm silencing my own
What I've left behind, Remember
Find my light Keep it bright
pass it on.
In you my spirit lives on
(Pause)
Find my light
pass it on. ◆

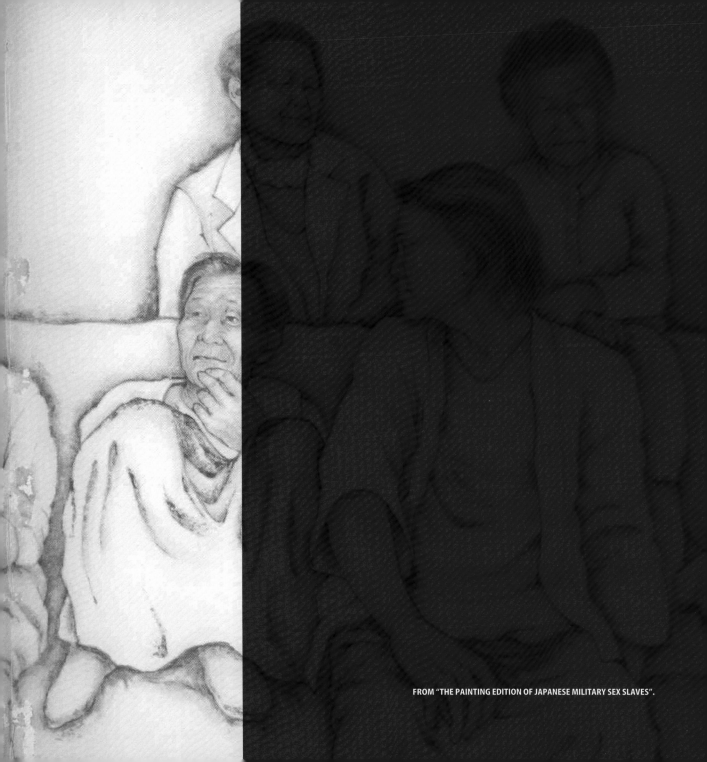

FROM "THE PAINTING EDITION OF JAPANESE MILITARY SEX SLAVES".

Japanese Military Sexual Slavery

Euphemized as "Comfort Women"

Tide Turning against Japanese Revisionists

The open denial statement given by Japanese Prime Minister Abe that there was no evidence to prove that the "Comfort Women" were coerced into sexual slavery had created an uproar and outcry from the victims, historians, institutions and world media.

2007 will go down in history as one of the most important watershed years for our long and difficult pursuit for truth and justice for WWII in Asia. It also happens to be the 70th Anniversary of the Rape of Nanking, and the 10th Anniversary of Iris Chang's book.

Besides the production and release of the docudrama of ' Iris Chang ', which is expected to be seen by hundreds of millions of people around the world, the education initiatives driven by Canada ALPHA has also inspired others in Asia and North America. The first ever study tour taking American teachers and educators to China was organized by our sister organizations in the United States in 2007.

But the most significant milestone probably is the rise of international attention to the ' comfort women ' issue. The open denial statement given by Japanese Prime Minister Abe that there was no evidence to prove that the ' comfort women ' were coerced into sexual slavery had created an uproar and outcry from the victims, historians, institutions and world media. The statement had proved to the world that the previous so-called apologies as claimed by the Japanese government, issued through different politicians, were both insincere and confusing. Such denial were further aggravated by the full page advertisement in the Washington Post in mid-June, signed by over 60 Japanese MPs and well-known right-wing historians and revisionists. Titled "The Facts", it had shamefully stated that the ' comfort women ' were not forced to be sex slaves because they earned a lot more than the Japanese soldiers and Army generals. This backfired badly on Japan and further confirmed that there has never been a serious attempt on Japan's part to confront its wartime crime and come to terms with history in a sensitive and sincere manner.

All these defensive actions by the Japanese government and the ring-wing revisionists were meant to suppress the passage of a pending Resolution in the American Congress. The Resolution 121, proposed by a California Congressman Michael Honda, a 3rd generation Japanese American, calls for the Japanese government to acknowledge and accept historical truth and responsibility, and formally apologize to the "Comfort Women" in a clear and unequivocal way.

Despite of the subsequent lobbying by the prime minister of Japan and the foreign minister, Resolution 121 was passed unanimously with full support of the Congress without a single doubt in July 2007. Such official condemnation on Japan's denial and continual whitewashing and distorting the history was the first in over 60 years after the war by the western world. Being the close and staunch allies as U.S. and Japan, this turn of event had proved to the world that 'truth and justice will prevail', and had given tremendous encouragement to the global movement to make Japan come to terms with its past.

Resolution 121 was passed unanimously with full support of the Congress without a single doubt in July 2007. Such official condemnation on Japan's denial and continual whitewashing and distorting the history was the first in over 60 years after the war by the western world.

Similar motions in the legislative chambers of different countries such as Australia, the Netherlands, and the Philippines have since initiated calling on Japan to sincerely deal with its wartime crimes.

In March 2007, Motion 291, similar to the Americans' Resolution 121, has been tabled in the Canadian House of Commons and had gathered continual support since then.

The initiative taken by Canada ALPHA to unite with the Korean, Filipino, and Indonesian communities in Canada to call on the Canadian House of Commons to pass Motion 291 is bearing fruit and gathering momentum from the communities. In 6 weeks' time during the summer of 2007, we got 40,000 Canadians signing the petition urging our MPs to support the Motion. So far we have got public endorsement from MPs and leaders of various political parties, and hope to gain support from more Canadian politicians who have a firm stand on the Canadian core value on humanity and human rights. With the full support from the community media and increasing awareness of the major media such as CBC, the Globe and Mail and the Toronto Star supporting our appeal, and publishing articles and editorials on the subject, we trust such an important human rights issue would finally gain support from both the Canadian public and the Parliament.

Plans are underway to bring "Comfort Women" victims from China, Korea, the Philippines and Netherlands to come to Canada to give testimonies to Canadians and the Parliament. We hope the live testimonies of these women who had gone through immeasurable pain and sufferings would raise the awareness of Canadians of such extreme brutality against women. The passing of Motion 291 would be a true reflection of Canadian value on justice and human rights.

Do not give up hope. Truth and justice will eventually reign. ◆

The passing of Motion 291 would be a true reflection of Canadian value on justice and human rights.

The Sex Slavery System
Under Japanese Militarism

Mianhuan Li
CHINA

TAKEN TO THE JAPANESE GARRISON IN JINGUISHE, SHANXI PROVINCE, IN 1943 AT AGE 16. RAPED BY THE CO AND BY SOLDIERS DURING THE DAY. AFTER 40 DAYS SHE WAS UNABLE TO WALK; HER FAMILY BOUGHT HER FREEDOM.

Suzuko Shirota
JAPAN

SOLD INTO PROSTITUTION TO PAY DEBTS. SENT TO A STATION IN TAIWAN IN 1939, AGE 18, THEN TO COAMFORT STATIONS IN THE SOUTH SEAS. AFTER THE WAR, SHE RAISED FUNDS TO BUILD MONUMENT TO DECEASED "COMFORT WOMEN."

Ines de Jesus
EAST TIMOR

TAKEN FROM A VILLAGE IN ERMERA TO BOBONARO. PUT TO HARD LABOR DURING THE DAY AND MADE A "COMFORT WOMAN" FOR JAPANESE SOLDIERS AT NIGHT. GAVE BIRTH IN THE COMFORT STATION BUT SOLDIERS TOOK HER BABY AWAY.

Yumin Deng
CHINA, "MIAO" TRIBE

DRAFTED AS A LABORER BUT RAPED BY THREE JAPANESE SOLDIERS AROUND 1943. HAD SHE ATTEMPTED ESCAPE, HER VILLAGE WOULD HAVE BEEN ASSAULTED. CONFINED IN A STORAGE HOUSE IN THE GARRISON FOR TWO YEARS.

Youliang Huang
CHINA

RAPED BY A JAPANESE SOLDIER AT HOME AT AGE 14. TAKEN TO GARRISONS AND COMFORT STATIONS. FORCED TO COOK DURING THE DAY AND RAPED AT NIGHT.

Rosalind Saw

MALAYSIA

TAKEN FROM HER TWO CHILDREN TO A COMFORT STATION BLINDFOLDED IN 1941 AT AGE 25. RAPED BY 60 SOLDIERS EVERYDAY WITH NO TIME EVEN TO DRESS. BORE A JAPANESE SOLDIER'S CHILD.

Ellen Corie van der Ploeg
THE NETHERLANDS

DETAINED IN THE HALMAHERA INTERNMENT CAMP, IN SEMARANG, INDONESIA, BY JAPANESE TROOPS IN 1942 AT AGE 19. SELECTED AS A "COMFORT WOMAN". CONTRACTED VD.

Jan Ruff-O'Herne
THE NETHERLANDS

DETAINED IN INTERNMENT CAMP FOR CIVILIANS IN 1942 AT AGE 19 AFTER THE JAPANESE INVADED JAVA. PUT IN A COMFORT STATION "THE HOUSE OF THE SEVEN SEAS" WITH 35 OTHER WOMEN.

Lintao Chen
CHINA

TAKEN TO JINGUISHE, SHANXI PROVINCE, IN 1943 AT AGE 20. TORTURED BECAUSE HER HUSBAND BELONGED TO THE EIGHTH ROUTE ARMY; HER THIGH WAS BROKEN. CONFINED AND RAPED IN A YAODONG FOR ABOUT TWENTY DAYS.

Geralda Cardoso
EAST TIMOR

ABDUCTED BY JAPANESE SOLDIERS IN HER VILLAGE IN COVA LIMA. TAKEN TO SUAI, BECO, AND BOBONARO, WHERE SHE WAS KEPT AS A "COMFORT WOMAN" FOR TWO YEARS. HARDLY GIVEN FOOD OR CLOTHING.

PHOTO BY YUNGHI KIM / CONTACT PRESS IMAGES / AMANAIMAGES

Article RUMIKO NISHINO, HAJIME KONDO
Photos YUNGHI KIM / CONTACT PRESS IMAGES /
AMANAIMAGES, JYUNJI WAKI, CONTRIBUTED BY
WOMEN'S ACTIVE MUSEUM ON WAR AND PEACE
Originally Published in DAYS JAPAN 2007

IN FRONT OF PON-NIM SON, A FORMER VICTIM OF JAPANESE MILITARY SEXUAL SLAV-ERY, A PAINTING BY KYOUNG-SHIN LEE DEPICTS HOW "MILITARY COMFORT WOMEN" WERE TAKEN FROM THEIR FAMILIES. IN ADJACENT BASEMENT APARTMENTS IN SEOUL, SOUTH KOREA, FOUR GRANDMOTHERS IN THEIR SEVENTIES LIVE CLOSE TOGETHER. (SEOUL, SOUTH KOREA. MARCH 1996.)

When faced with criticism by China and other countries on this issue, many in Japan have chosen to ignore or dismiss such accusations as "anti-Japanese propaganda." However, the public testimony in recent years of 100 women (of the 200,000 sex slaves recognized by the United Nations) who were once forced into sexual slavery show just how such ignorance has deprived the women of their dignity during the more than 60 years since the war ended. The astounding testimony of a former Japanese soldier, featured here, exposes the reality of the rapes and other barbarous acts committed against women by Japanese military men. The testimony of the 100 women themselves provides us with an opportunity to begin sharing in the healing — and to start truly facing history.

Du-Ri Park
SOUTH KOREA

DECEIVED AND TAKEN TO A COMFORT STATION IN CHANGHUA, TAIWAN IN 1940 AT AGE 17. NAMED "FUJIKO" AND FORCED TO BE A COMFORT WOMAN FOR FIVE YEARS UNTIL THE WAR ENDED.

Won-Ok Gil
SOUTH KOREA

TAKEN TO A COMFORT STATION IN HARBIN, NORTHEASTERN CHINA, IN 1940 AT AGE 13. DUE TO HER YOUTH, SHE WAS TERRIFIED OF JAPANESE SOLDIERS. CONTRACTED SEVERE VENEREAL DISEASE.

Sang-Hee Kim
SOUTH KOREA

ABDUCTED IN 1935 AT AGE 16 ON THE WAY TO DAEGU TO HAVE PAHOTOS TAKEN. FORCED TO BE A "COMFORT WOMAN" FOR TEN YEARS IN SHANGHAI, NANKING, SINGAPORE, ETC.

Kun-Ja Kim ▸
SOUTH KOREA

DECEIVED AND TAKEN TO A COMFORT STATION IN HUICHUN, CHINA IN 1942 AT AGE 16. FORCED TO SERVICE AS MANY AS 40 SOLDIERS A DAY. RESISTANCE WAS MET WITH A BEATING THAT RUPTURED HER RIGHT EARDRUM.

Duk-Kyung Kang
SOUTH KOREA

WENT AT AGE 16 TO THE FUJIKOSHI FACTORY IN TOYAMA, JAPAN, IN 1944, WITH THE WOMEN'S VOLUNTEER LABOR CORPS. FLED DUE TO HARSH CONDITIONS, BUT AN MP CAPTURED HER AND FORCED TO BE A "COMFORT WOMAN."

Ok-Seon Park
SOUTH KOREA

CAPTURED BY JAPANESE MEN WHILE DRAWING WATER IN 1941 AT AGE 17 AND SENT TO A COMFORT STATION IN MULING, NORTHEASTERN CHINA. ESCAPED WHEN THE SOVIET ARMY ATTACKED IN 1945.

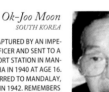

Hyun-Soon Shin
SOUTH KOREA

TAKEN TO PAPUA NEW GUINEA IN 1941 AT AGE 17 AFTER BEING PROMISED A NURSING JOB. RELOCATEDLATER TO A NAVY COMFORT STATION IN RANGOON. SHE BECAME A NUN AFTER THE WAR.

Jok-Gan Bae
SOUTH KOREA

ORDERED TO WORK IN A SPINNING FACTORY BY THE GROUP LEADER AND WARD HEAD OF HER VILLAGE IN 1938 AT AGE 17; TAKEN TO A COMFORT STATION IN HANGCHOW (NOW HANGZHOU), CHINA. GIVEN IDENTIFICATION NUMBER 33.

Yong-Nyeo Lee
SOUTH KOREA

DECEIVED AND TAKEN TO BURMA IN 1942 AT AGE 16. ONE YEAR LATER SHE WAS TRANSFERRED TO A UNIT STATIONED DEEP IN THE MOUNTAINS. PUT INTO A POW CAMP IN RANGOON AFTER THE WAR.

Ok-Joo Moon
SOUTH KOREA

CAPTURED BY AN IMPERIAL OFFICER AND SENT TO A COMFORT STATION IN MANCHURIA IN 1940 AT AGE 16. TRANSFERRED TO MANDALAY, BURMA IN 1942. REMEMBERS SOLDIERS WAITING IN LINE FOR THEIR TURN.

Bok-Dong Kim
SOUTH KOREA

ORDERED TO JOIN THE WOMEN'S VOLUNTEER CORPS, SHE WAS SENT INSTEAD TO A COMFORT STATION IN GUANGDONG IN 1941 AT AGE 16. GUARDS STATIONED AT THE GATE BLOCKED ESCAPE. ATTEMPTED SUICIDE BUT FAILED.

Soon-Duk Kim
SOUTH KOREA

PROMISED "FACTORY WORK," BUT TAKEN INSTEAD TO A COMFORT STATION IN SHANGHAI IN 1937 AT AGE 16. FORCED TO SERVICE UP TO 30 TO 40 MEN A DAY, INCLUDING HIGH-RANKING MILITARY OFFICIALS.

Ok-Seon Lee
SOUTH KOREA

CAPTURED WHILE SHOPPING AND SENT TO A COMFORT STATION IN YANJI, NORTHEASTERN CHINA IN 1942 AT AGE 15. AFTER A FAILED ESCAPE ATTEMPT, SEVERELY BEATEN AND TORTURED.

Dal-Yeon Shim
SOUTH KOREA

KIDNAPPED IN A FIELD AT AGE 12 OR 13 AND TAKEN TO AN EXTREMELY COLD REGION OF NORTHEASTERN CHINA. FORCED TO SERVE AS A COMFORT WOMAN FOR TROOPS AT THE FRONT. REPATRIATED AFTER WAR.

Bun-Seon Kim
SOUTH KOREA

PROMISED WORK IN A FACTORY, SHE WAS TAKEN INSTEAD TO A COMFORT STATION IN TAIWAN IN 1937 AT AGE 15. LATER TRANSFERRED TO MANILA. SHE HAD BEEN FORCED TO LEARN THE "OATH OF IMPERIAL SUBJECTS" BY HEART.

Pil-Gi Moon
SOUTH KOREA

DECEIVED AND TAKEN TO A COMFORT STATION IN MANCHURIA IN 1943 AT AGE 18. THE 30 KOREAN WOMEN THERE WERE BEATEN AND THREATENED WITH A SABER IF THEY RESISTED.

Yong-Soo Lee
SOUTH KOREA

TAKEN TO A COMFORT STATION IN HSINCHU, TAIWAN IN 1944 AT AGE 16. A HANGING BLANKET MARKED HER ROOM'S ENTRANCE. RAPE CONTINUED DURING MENSTRUATION.

Hak-Soon Kim
SOUTH KOREA

ABDUCTED BY JAPANESE SOLDIERS FROM A RESTAURANT IN BEIJING, THROWN INTO A TRUCK AND TAKEN TO A COMFORT STATION IN 1941 AT AGE 17. THE FIRST SURVIVOR TO SPEAK OUT. SUED THE GOVERNMENT OF JAPAN IN 1991.

Ok-Ryeon Park
SOUTH KOREA

ANSWERED AN AD FOR A "CONSOLATION PARTY" IN 1941 AT AGE 23; INSTEAD TAKEN TO A COMFORT STATION IN RABAUL. FORBIDDEN TO SPEAK KOREAN.

Soon-Ae Kang
SOUTH KOREA

MILITARY POLICE AND POLICE OFFICERS CAME TO HER HOUSE, AND TOOK AWAY AND SENT HER TO TROOPS AT HIROSHIMA VIA PUSAN AND SHIMONOSEKI. LATER INTERNED IN A COMFORT STATION IN PALAU. REPATRIATED IN 1946.

Geum-Joo Hwang *SOUTH KOREA*

DECEIVED AND SENT TO A COMFORT STATION IN JILIN, NORTHEASTERN CHINA, IN 1941 AT AGE 20. "COMFORT WOMEN" WITH SEVERE VENEREAL DISEASE WERE TAKEN AWAY BY JAPANESE SOLDIERS AND NEVER CAME BACK.

Soon-Ok Kim
SOUTH KOREA

TRICKED AND TAKEN TO A COMFORT STATION IN DONGNING, NORTHEASTERN CHINA IN 1942 AT AGE 20. NAMED "KAYOKO" AND FORCED TO SERVICE OFFICERS.

Sang-ok Lee
NORTH KOREA

ORDERED TO "CONTRIBUTE HER VIRGINITY" TO THE WAR EFFORT, SENT TO A COMFORT STATION NEAR SOONCHON, PYONGYANNAM-DO IN 1943 AT AGE 17. FORCED TO SERVE 20 TO 25 MEN A DAY, LIKE A CONVICT IN JAIL.

Maxima Regala de la Cruz
THE PHILIPPINES

CAPTURED BY JAPANESE SOLDIERS ALONG WITH HER MOTHER WHILE IN THE MARKET OF SAN ILDEFONSO AND TAKEN TO THEIR GARRISON IN 1944 AT AGE 14. IMPRISONED AND RAPED EVERYDAY FOR THREE MONTHS.

Justina Villanueva Pido
THE PHILIPPINES

RAPED BY A JAPANESE SOLDIER NAMED YAMATO WHILE WORKING IN THE MARKET IN NEGROS AROUND 1942 AT AGE 21. CONFINED IN THE JAPANESE GARRISON ABOUT 10 MONTHS. SHE BORE YAMATO'S BABY.

Bok-Seon Kim
SOUTH KOREA

PROMISED A JOB AT A JAPANESE FACTORY IN 1944 AT AGE 18, TAKEN FROM OSAKA, VIA SAIGON, TO BURMA. ESCAPED AND WANDERED THROUGH THE JUNGLE UNTIL SHE WAS TAKEN CAPTIVE.

Yong-suk Kim
NORTH KOREA

DECEIVED BY A JAPANESE POLICEMAN AND TAKEN TO A COMFORT STATION IN SHENYANG, CHINA IN 1940 AT AGE 13. DUE TO HER EXTREME YOUTH AND PHYSICAL IMMATURITY, HER GENITALS WERE CUT OPEN BY A JAPANESE SOLDIER.

Yong-sim Pak
NORTH KOREA

DECEIVED AND TAKEN TO A COMFORT STATION IN NANJING IN 1939 AT AGE 17. TRANSFERRED AFTERWARDS TO BURMA AND LAMENG, YUNNAN PROVINCE, CHINA. WAS HEAVILY PREGNANT WHEN TAKEN CAPTIVE BY THE CHINESE ARMY.

Januaria Galang Garcia
THE PHILIPPINES

HER VILLAGE, MAPANIQUE, WAS RAIDED IN THE JAPANESE MILITARY GUERILLA CLEAN UP OPERATION ON NOVEMBER 23, 1944, AND SET ON FIRE SHE WAS GANG RAPED IN THE RED HOUSE WITH WOMEN AND GIRLS AT AGE 14.

Rosita P. Nasino
THE PHILIPPINES

ABDUCTED ON HER WAY TO HER GRANDMOTHER'S HOME ON PANAI ISLAND IN 1943 AT AGE 15. IMPRISONED IN THE GARRISON AND GANG RAPED. ABOUT 10 WOMEN ENDURED THE SAME ORDEAL.

Sang-Sook Ha
SOUTH KOREA

DECEIVED AND TAKEN TO A COMFORT STATION COMPOUND CALLED "JIQINGLI," IN WUHAN, CHINA IN 1944 AT AGE 17. REPATRIATED 58 YEARS LATER BUT, UNABLE TO RE-ADAPT, RETURNED TO CHINA IN 2005.

Kae-wol Lee
NORTH KOREA

BY DECEPTION TAKEN TO A COMFORT STATION NEAR HARBIN IN 1937 AT AGE 15. WHEN SHE RESISTED, BURNING CIGARETTES WERE PRESSED INTO HER SKIN. ESCAPED 2 YEARS LATER.

Bong-gi Bae
SOUTH KOREA
RESIDENT IN JAPAN

OFFERED A JOB BY WOMEN BROKERS IN 1943 AT AGE 29. TAKEN BY MILITARY TRANSPORT SHIP FROM PUSAN TO TOKASHIKI ISLAND, OKINAWA, PUT IN A COMFORT STATION. REMAINED IN OKINAWA AFTER THE WAR.

Tomasa Salinog
THE PHILIPPINES

ON PANAY ISLAND CAPTAIN "HIRO'OKA" ABDUCTED HER AFTER BEHEADING HER FATHER IN 1942. SHE WAS 13. CONFINED AND MADE A SEX SLAVE. REJECTED THE AWF.

Sabina Villegas
THE PHILIPPINES

HER FATHER WAS KILLED DURING THE RAID AGAINST THEIR MOUNTAIN VILLAGE IN LUZON IN 1942 16. IMPRISONED AND RAPED IN THE GARRISON WITH HER SISTERS. THE SISTERS WERE RELEASED AFTER CONTRACTING MALARIA.

Il-Chool Kanh
SOUTH KOREA

TAKEN AWAY BY JAPANESE POLICE IN HER PARENTS' ABSENCE. TRANSPORTED TO A COMFORT STATION IN MUDANJIANG,CHINA, IN 1943 AT AGE 16. ENDURED NUMEROUS INJECTIONS FOR THE TREATMENT OF VENEREAL DISEASE.

Kum-nyo Kwak
NORTH KOREA

DECEIVED AND TAKEN TO A COMFORT STATION IN MULING, NORTHEASTERN CHINA IN 1939. BEATINGS FOR RESISTANCE RESULTED IN A BROKEN WRIST. .TAKING ADVANTAGE OF A LIGHTLY GUARDED OCCASION, SHE ESCAPED 2 YEARS LATER.

Shin-do Song
SOUTH KOREA
RESIDENT IN JAPAN

TRICKED AND TAKEN TO "SEKAIKAN" STATION, WUCHANG, CHINA IN 1938 AT AGE 16. EXPERIENCED SEVERAL PREGNANCIES AND BIRTHS. AFTER THE WAR, SHE WAS DECEIVED BY A JAPANESE SOLDIER AND BROUGHT TO JAPAN.

Juanita Jamot
THE PHILIPPINES

DRAGGED FROM HOME IN MANILA IN1944, WHEN SHE WAS ABOUT 20 AND PREGNANT. CONFINED AND RAPED FOR ABOUT A MONTH. LEFT FOR DEAD, SHE SURVIVED A MASSACRE IN A CHURCH.

Cristita D. Alcober
THE PHILIPPINES

FORCIBLY CONSCRIPTED WITH 30 OTHER WOMEN AND GIRLS FROM VILLAGES ON LEYTE ISLAND AROUND 1942, AT AGE 16. CONFINED TO THE GARRISON FOR 2 YEARS, DIGGING TRENCHES DURING THE DAY AND SERVING AS A SEX SLAVE AT NIGHT.

Rufina Fernandez
THE PHILIPPINES

HER FATHER, MOTHER, AND FOUR SISTERS WERE KILLED IN A SWEEP-UP OPERATION IN MANILA IN 1944. IMPRISONED IN THE GARRISON AND GANG RAPED FOR 3 MONTHS AT AGE 17. BEARS A LONG SCAR FROM A SABER ON HER RIGHT SHOULDER.

Felicidad de los Reyes
THE PHILIPPINES

AFTER A WELCOME CEREMONY FOR THE JAPANESE ARMY ON MASBATE ISLAND IN 1943, TEACHER TOLD THE STUDENTS TO COME RECEIVE TOYS. THE SOLDIERS THEN TOOK HER, AGED 14, AND OTHERS TO THE GARRISON AND GANG RAPED.

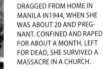

Remedios Valencia
THE PHILIPPINES

ABDUCTED FROM THE MARKET IN MANILA AND GANG RAPED AT AGE 22 IN 1943. HER SISTER WAS KILLED. IMPRISONED FOR ALMOST ONE YEAR. REPEATEDLY RAPED DAY AND NIGHT. UNDERWENT MEDICAL CHECKS FOR VENEREAL DISEASE.

Hsiu-mei Wu
TAIWAN

SHE WENT TO GUANDONG IN 1940 AT AGE 23 WITH HER HUSBAND, A RESTAURANT OWNER WHO WAS ORDERED BY THE POLICE TO OPEN AN EATERY THERE. NAMED "KIYOKO" AND FORCED TO WORK AS A "COMFORT WOMAN" AT THE FRONT.

A-tao Huang
SOUTH KOREA

PROMISED A JOB AS ASSISTANT NURSE OR COOK, SHE WAS TAKEN TO BALIKPAPAN, INDONESIA IN 1942 AT AGE 19. INJURED IN THE ABDOMEN IN AN AIR RAID.

Anastacia Cortez
THE PHILIPPINES

ARRESTED AT HOME IN MANILA IN 1944 AT AGE 19 WITH HER HUSBAND WHO HAD ESCAPED FROM A PRISONER CAMP. BECAME PREGNANT DURING 5-MONTH OF IMPRISONMENT BUT LATER MISCARRIED. HER HUSBAND WAS KILLED.

Hilaria Bustamante
THE PHILIPPINES

THROWN INTO A MILITARY TRUCK FROM THE STATE ROAD ON LUZON ISLAND AND TAKEN TO THE GARRISON IN 1943 AT AGE 17. GANG RAPED WITH 3 OTHER GIRLS FOR 13 MONTHS. FORCED TO COOK AND DO LAUNDRY.

Pilar F. Frias
THE PHILIPPINES

GANG RAPED AND SLASHED ACROSS THE NOSE IN LUZON ISLAND IN 1942, AT AGE 16. ABDUCTED IN 1944. SHE AND 3 OTHER WOMEN WERE TIED TOGETHER AT THE WAIST, TAKEN THROUGH THE JUNGLE AND GANG RAPED REPEATEDLY FOR 2 MONTHS.

Umin Shobai
TAIWAN, "TAROKO" TRIBE

IN 1944, SHE AND HER THREE CHILDREN WERE ORDERED BY POLICE OFFICER TAKIMURA TO WORK FOR JAPANESE TROOPS. A 31-YEAR-OLD WIDOW, SHE WAS LATER RAPED, BECAME PREGNANT AND HAD A BABY.

Man-mei Lu
TAIWAN

DECEIVED BY THE PROMISE OF A BETTER JOB AND TAKEN TO HAINAN ISLAND IN 1943 AT AGE 17. HELD UNTIL SHE WAS 8 MONTHS PREGNANT, THEN RELEASED AND SENT HOME. HER BABY DIED 38 DAYS AFTER BIRTH.

Maria R. L. Henson
THE PHILIPPINES

GANG RAPED BY JAPANESE SOLDIERS IN LUZON IN 1942 AT AGE 14. CAPTURED IN 1943; GANG RAPED AND TORTURED FOR 9 MONTHS. REPEATED ASSAULTS DEFORMED HER MOUTH AND JAW. FIRST SURVIVOR FROM THE PHILIPPINES TO TESTIFY.

Piedad N. Nobleza
THE PHILIPPINES

TAKEN TO THE GARRISON IN NORTHERNPANAY ISLAND IN 1943 AT AGE 22. DETAINED THERE WITH MORE THAN 10 WOMEN FOR ABOUT 2 WEEKS ANDGANG RAPED EVERY NIGHT.

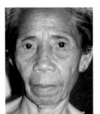

Felicitas Jampolina
THE PHILIPPINES

WHEN HER HOME ON LUZON ISLAND WAS RAIDED IN 1944, SHE WAS TAKEN TO THE GARRISON AT AGE 10 BEFORE HER FIRST MENSTRUATION. IMPRISONED AND RAPED THERE WITH OTHER 10 GIRLS. ESCAPED SIX WEEKS LATER.

Kuei-ying Tsai
TAIWAN

OFFERED A "JOB AS A WAITRESS," SHE WAS INSTEAD TAKEN WITH HER SISTER TO A STATION ON HAIAN ISLAND IN 1943 AT AGE 18. LATER SUFFERED INFLAMMATION OF THE WOMB AND, UNABLE TO WORK, WAS RELEASED AND SENT HOME.

Yin-chiao Su
TAIWAN

DECEIVED BY THE PROMISE OF A JOB, TAKEN WITH HER YOUNGER SISTER TO HAINAN ISLAND IN 1943 AT AGE 20. SHE BECAME SO SICK THAT SHE WAS FINALLY RELEASED AND RETURNED TO TAIWAN.

Rosario Nopueto
THE PHILIPPINES

ABOUT 30 VILLAGERS ON PANAY ISLAND INCLUDING HER FATHER AND SISTER WERE KILLED IN 1944. SHE WAS DETAINED AND RAPED IN THE GARRISON FOR 3 MONTHS AT AGE 18 AND WAS ALMOST KILLED JUST BEFORE US FORCES LANDED.

N. Gertrude M. Balisalisa
THE PHILIPPINES

TAKEN FROM HER HOME ON LUZON ISLAND IN 1944 AT AGE 24. FORCED TO SERVE OFFICER KOBAYASHI AS A "COMFORT WOMAN". DETAINED IN THE GARRISON FOR 14 MONTHS AND RAPED REPEATEDLY BY OFFICERS.

Lucia Misa
THE PHILIPPINES

HER PARENTS AND SISTER WERE SLAUGHTERED AT HOME ON LUZON ISLAND IN 1944 WHEN SHE WAS 15. THEN TAKEN TO THE GARRISON. CONFINED AND GANG RAPED WITH 14 OTHER WOMEN AND GIRLS. ESCAPED THREE MONTHS LATER.

Anika
TAIWAN, "BUNUN" TRIBE

AT AGE 21 IN 1942, SHE WAS TOLD SHE WAS GOING TO MEET HER NEWLY-WED HUSBAND, BUT TAKEN INSTEAD TO HONG KONG. SERVED HIGH-RANKING OFFICERS DURING THE DAY AND WAS RAPED AT NIGHT. BECAME PREGNANT BUT MISCARRIED.

Ubusu Rabai
TAIWAN, "TAROKO" TRIBE

ORDERED BY TAGUCHI FROM THE LOCAL POLICE STATION TO WORK FOR THE JAPANESE TROOPS IN 1944 AT AGE 15. SHE WAS RAPED REPEATEDLY BY SOLDIERS, AND LATER BECAME PREGNANT AND HAD A BABY.

Bao-zhu Gao
TAIWAN

TOLD TO "SERVE" THE JAPA-NESE MILITARY IN KWANTUNG (GUANGDONG), SHE WAS SENT THERE AT AGE 17, THEN TRANSFERRED TO BURMA. RAPE CONTINUED UNTIL THE 8TH MONTH OF HER PREG-NANCY. SHE RETURNED HOME VIA VIETNAM.

Apai Iyan
TAIWAN, "TAROKO" TRIBE

ORDERED BY TAKEMURA, A JAPANESE POLICEMAN, TO DO CHORES FOR JAPA-NESE TROOPS IN 1944 AT AGE 17. SHE WAS LATER FORCED TO BE A "COMFORT WOMAN" AND EXPERIENC-ED SEVERAL PREGNANCIES AND MISCARRIAGES.

Erpu Nan
CHINA

ABDUCTED IN 1942 AT AGE 19 FROM HEDONG, SHANXI PROVINCE AND FORCED TO BE A "COMFORT WOMEN". HAD A BABY. AFTER THE WAR, SHE WAS TRIED AS A COLLABORATOR WITH JAPAN. COMMITTED SUICIDE IN 1967.

Xihe Yang
CHINA

REPEATEDLY RAPED BY TWO JAPANESE SOLDIERS IN HER PARENTS' HOUSE IN HEDONG, SHANXI PROVINCE BETWEEN 1942 AND 1943. SUFFERED IN SILENCE UNTIL SPEAKING OUT FOR JUSTICE SIX MONTHS BEFORE HER DEATH.

Runmei Zhao
CHINA

AT AGE 16 SHE WAS ABDUCTED IN FRONT OF HER FOSTER-PARENTS. GANG RAPED FOR 40 DAYS AT THE HEDONG BATTERY, SHANXI PROVINCE. SUFFERED FROM INFERTILITY AND SEVERE PTSD.

Umau Rapin
TAIWAN, "TAROKO" TRIBE

FORCED TO DO CHORES FOR THE JAPANESE TROOPS IN 1944, WHEN SHE WAS 16. ABOUT ONE MONTH LATER SHE WAS FORCED TO BE A "COMFORT WOMAN," BECAME PREGNANT, AND HAD A BABY DAUGHTER.

Tanaha Iwar
TAIWAN, "TAROKO" TRIBE

ORDERED BY TSUBAKI, A JAPANESE POLICE OFFICER, TO DO CHORES FOR THE TROOPS IN 1944 AT AGE 13. LATER FORCED TO BE A "COMFORT WOMAN". EXPERI-ENCED REPEATED PREGNAN-CIES AND MISCARRIAGES.

Gaihe Wang
CHINA

HER HUSBAND, THEN VIL-LAGE MAYOR, WAS KILLED IN 1942. TAKEN TO THE HEDONG BATTERY, SHANXI PROVINCE, WHERE SHE WAS RAPED AND TORTURED EVERYDAY, AT AGE 23. STILL SUFFERS BOTH PHYSICALLY AND PSYCHOLOGICALLY.

Shizhen Yang
CHINA

GANG RAPED BY JAPANESE SOLDIERS IN HEDONG, SHANXI PROVINCE IN 1941 OR 1942. FORCED TO BE A SEX SLAVE FOR NONCOM-MISSIONED OFFICERS ONLY. STILL SUFFERS FROM THE AFTEREFFECTS OF THE ATROCITIES.

Yulin Yin
CHINA

LOST HER HUSBAND TO ILL-NESS AT AGE 19. GANG RAPED BY JAPANESE SOLDIERS IN SHANXI PROVINCE AT DAY AND NIGHT. SHE SUF-FERED FROM AFTEREFFECTS SUCH AS MENSTRUAL IRREGU-LARITIES AND PALSY.

Chen-tao Chen
TAIWAN

ABDUCTED BY A JAPANESE POLICE OFFICER ON HER WAY TO SCHOOL IN 1942 AT AGE 19. SENT FROM KAOHSIUNG TO THE ANDA-MAN ISLANDS IN THE INDIAN OCEAN. RETURNED HOME FOUR MONTHS PREGNANT BUT LOST THE BABY.

Yang Chen
TAIWAN

PROMISED A JOB AS A "WAITRESS IN A RESTAURANT," SHE WENT TO BURMA IN 1943 AT AGE 21. WITHIN A WEEK FORCED TO BE A "COMFORT WOMAN". WHEN SHE RE-FUSED, THE MANAGER HIT HER SO HARD THAT HER EARDRUM RUPTURED.

Yin'e Gao
CHINA

EXPERIENCED THE NANSHE MASSACRE INCIDENT, SHANXI PROVINCE IN 1941 AT AGE 16. TAKEN TO THE A BATTERY IN THE VILLAGE OF HEDONG WITH OTHERS AND CONFINED THERE. RAPED EVERYDAY. LATER DIVORCED DUE TO INFERTILITY.

Cunni Zhao
CHINA

CAPTURED AND TAKEN TO THE XIYAN BATTERY BY THE JAPANESE ARMY DURING THEIR ATTACK ON YAOSHAN VILLAGE, SHANXI PROVINCE IN 1942 AT AGE 24. CON-FINED AND GANG RAPED EVERYDAY. HER BOUND FEET PREVENTED ESCAPE.

Jinyu Chen
CHINA, "LI" TRIBE

WHEN SHE WAS 14, JAPA-NESE SOLDIERS BROKE INTO HER HOME AND RAPED HER IN FRONT OF HER PARENTS. SHE WAS — FORCED TO COMMUTE TO THE GARRISON AFTERWARDS AND GANG RAPED REPEATEDLY.

Chuen Lee
TAIWAN

IN 1942 AT AGE 22, SHE APPLIED TO DRAW LOTS FOR A JOB OPENING ORGANIZED BY THE DISTRICT OFFICE, BUT WAS TAKEN TO THE PHILIPPINES. SHE WAS BATTERED AND BEATEN BY SOLDIERS UNTIL HER EARDRUM RUPTURED.

Kage Toyo
TAIWAN, "TAIYARU" TRIBE

ORDERED BY KAWAHADA, A JAPANESE POLICE OFFICER, TO DO CHORES FOR JAPANESE TROOPS IN 1943 AT AGE 16. ABOUT A MONTH LATER, FORCED TO BE A "COMFORT WOMAN." BECAME PREGNANT BUT MISCARRIED.

Xiantu Zhang
CHINA

THE JAPANESE ARMY RAIDED XIYAN IN 1942 WHEN SHE WAS 15. ABDUCTED AND FORCIBLY TAKEN INTO A YAODONG AT THE HEDONG BATTERY, AND REPEATEDLY GANG RAPED BY A DOZEN JAPANESE SOLDIERS FOR 20 DAYS.

Aihua Wan
CHINA

JOINED THE ANTI-JAPANESE RESISTANCE IN 1942 AT AGE 12. CAPTURED THREE TIMES. TORTURED AND GANG RAPED AT JINGUISHE, SHANXI PROVINCE. FIRST CHINESE SURVIVOR TO SPEAK OUT ABOUT WARTIME SEXUAL SLAVERY.

Yabian Chen
CHINA, "LI" TRIBE

TAKEN TO A JAPANESE ARMY GARRISON AT AGE 14, THEN CONFINED IN A COMFORT STATION AT TENGQIAO. AFTER THE WAR JAPAN'S DEFEAT, SHE HID IN THE MOUNTAINS FOR A MONTH.

Yadong Tan
CHINA, "LI" TRIBE

AT AGE 16 OR 17 SHE WAS TAKEN TO A GARRISON ON THE PRETEXT THAT SHE WOULD "SERVE JAPANESE SOLDIERS." SHE WAS IMPRISONED AND RAPED. SHE LOST HER HEARING IN ONE EAR DUE TO VIOLENT TREATMENT.

Mianhuan Li
CHINA

TAKEN TO THE JAPANESE GARRISON IN JINGUISHE, SHANXI PROVINCE, IN 1943 AT AGE 16. RAPED BY THE CO AND BY SOLDIERS DURING THE DAY. AFTER 40 DAYS SHE WAS UNABLE TO WALK; HER FAMILY BOUGHT HER FREEDOM.

Xicui Guo
CHINA

TAKEN TO JINGUISHE, SHANXI PROVINCE, IN 1942 AT AGE 15 WITH HER OLDER SISTER'S FAMILY. CONFINED AND RAPED FOR TWO WEEKS. RETURNED TO FAMILY, BUT LATER ABDUCTED TWICE. BEDRIDDEN FOR FIVE YEARS AFTER THE WAR.

Mardiyem
INDONESIA

PROMISED SHE WOULD BE AN ACTRESS, SHE WAS TAKEN FROM JAVA IN 1943 AT AGE 13 TO A COMFORT STATION IN BORNEO. GOT PREGNANT AT AGE 14 BUT HAD AN ABORTION, BUT RAPES RESUMED SOON AFTERWARDS.

Esmeralda Boe
EAST TIMOR

RAPED AT AGE 12 OR 13 AT THE HOUSE OF A JAPANESE OFFICER IN MEMO, HER VILLAGE. MADE A "COMFORT WOMAN" EXCLUSIVELY FOR OFFICERS UEMURA, HARUKU AND KAWANO FOR TWO YEARS.

Yajin Lin
CHINA, "LI" TRIBE

SEIZED BY JAPANESE SOLDIERS IN 1943; TAKEN TO THEIR GARRISON WITH HER HANDS TIED BEHIND HER BACK. RAPED EVERYDAY THERE, AND TORTURED WITH BURNING CIGARETTE BUTTS.

Qiaolian Hou
CHINA

TAKEN TO THE JAPANESE GARRISON IN JINGUISHE, SHANXI PROVINCE, IN 1942 AT AGE 14, WITH HER FATHER AND FIVE OTHER WOMEN. RAPED. RELEASED AFTER ABOUT 40 DAYS IN EXCHANGE FOR SILVER. SUFFERS SEVERE PTSD.

Xixiang Zhou
CHINA

ABDUCTED WHILE ACTING FOR THE ANTI-JAPAN WOMEN'S SALVATION ASSOCIATION IN 1944 AT AGE 19. CONFINED, RAPED AND TORTURED IN JINGUISHE, SHANXI PROVINCE. RESCUED BY THE EIGHTH ROUTE ARMY EN ROUTE TO HER EXECUTION.

Suhanah
INDONESIA

TAKEN BY 6 JAPANESE SOLDIERS IN FRONT OF HER HOUSE NEAR BANDONG, JAVA AT AGE 16, 1942. CONFINED IN A COMFORT STATION EXCLUSIVELY FOR JAPANESE SOLDIERS AND OFFICERS UNTIL THE END OF THE WAR.

Marta Abu Bere
EAST TIMOR

TAKEN FROM A VILLAGE IN BOBONARO PREFECTURE TO MAROBO, A HOT-SPRING RESORT, AND MADE A "COMFORT WOMAN." FORCED TO WORK DURING THE DAY, RAPED BY JAPANESE SOLDIERS AT NIGHT, BEFORE HER FIRST MENSTRUATION…

Duk-Kyung Kang
INNOCENCE STOLEN, 87X130
ACRYLIC ON CANVAS, 1995

일본군 '성노예'
피해할머니 작품집

The Painting Edition of
Japanese Military Sexual Slaves

日本軍「性奴隷」被害生存女性の絵画集

Il Chul Kang
BURNING VIRGINS, 72.5X60.5 ACRYLIC ON CANVAS, 2002

Soon–Duk Kim
[LEFT] IN THAT PLACE, AT THAT MOMENT IN TIME 2,
39X53, ACRYLIC ON PAPER, 1995 **[RIGHT]** STOLEN
AWAY, 115X114.5, ACRYLIC ON CANVAS, 1995

Duk-Kyung Kang
[LEFT] BITTERNESS OF COMFORT WOMEN'S
GHOSTS, 64X47, ACRYLIC ON PAPER, 1995 **[RIGHT]**
UNTITLED, 45X53, ACRYLIC ON PAPER, 1996

U.S. Resolution 121

Canada's Motion 291

Ever since the massacre, there has been a gaping hole of social injustice that the Chinese population feel indignant about. Lately, there has been an international movement not only in China but also in other countries as well such as the United States, Korea, Canada, Holland, and the Philippines. In America, the congress has passed resolution 121 which asks that the Japanese government apologize to the comfort women and include a curriculum about them in schools. This bill was passed on July 30, 2007. In Canada, the Chinese community is lobbying towards establishing Motion 291 which urges the Canadian government to ask the Japanese to formally apologize to the women who were coerced into military sexual slavery during the Second World War and were euphemized as "Comfort Women", and also to provide honourable compensation to these victims. So far, the only statement close to an apology from

Japan is the "Kono Statement" made by Yohei Kono in 1993. It was admitted that the military played a central role in coercing women to become sex slaves, but only after a Japanese historian discovered such records in buried military documents in Japan. However, this statement was not approved by the Japanese parliament and there is a lack of evidence to prove there was such coercion.

United States House of Representatives House Resolution 121 is a Resolution about comfort women which Mike Honda intoduced to the American House of Representatives in 2007. It asks that the Japanese government apologize to comfort women and include curriculum about them in schools. This bill was passed on July 30, 2007.

In Canada parliamentary Motion 291 statesThat, in the opinion of the House, the government should urge the Prime Minister and the Parliament of Japan to: (a) pass a resolution in the Diet to formally apologize to the women who were coerced into military sexual slavery during the Second World War and were euphemized as "Comfort Women" by the Japanese Imperial Army; and (b) to provide just and honorable compensation to these victims.

KOREAN 'CW' VICTIM AND COMMUNITY IN PRESS CONFERENCE RIGHT AFTER THE UNANIMOUS PASSAGE OF HR121 AT US CONGRESS.

ALPHA AND MICHAEL M. HONDA.

U. S. CONGRESSMAN ENI FALEO-
MAVAEGA WITH CANADA ALPHA
REPRESENTATIVES FLORA CHONG
AND DR. JOSEPH Y. K. WONG.

Petition To The House Of Commons Concerning "Comfort Women" Motion M-291

We, the undersigned residents of Canada, draw the attention of the House of Commons to the following:

WHEREAS: For over 60 years, the young women who were forced into sexual slavery lived with the shame attached to the ordeal. This caused many to conceal their past and only recently a few of them have come forward and speak out against the atrocities they experienced. For too long, this dark spot of history has been largely glossed over or ignored by Japan.

WHEREAS: As a friend and ally of Japan, Canada should urge the Government of Japan to acknowledge and accept the responsibility for its past actions as it attempts to maintain a good relationship with its neighbors in the Pacific and with Canada.

WHEREAS: Human rights are universal and transcend geographic boundaries. As a member of the international community in good standing, Canada has been loud and clear in condemnation of human rights violations wherever they occur. As Canadians, we are proud of and applaud our government's firm expression of our Canadian values.

WHEREAS: The Member of Parliament for Trinity-Spadina, has presented to the House of Commons motion M-291 which reads as follows: That, in the opinion of the House, the government should urge the Prime Minister and the Parliament of Japan to: (a) pass a resolution in the Diet to formally apologize to the women who were coerced into military sexual slavery during the Second World War and were euphemized as "comfort women" by the Japanese Imperial Army; and (b) provide just and honorable compensation to these victims.

WHEREAS: Only through action of the international community, such as the passing of Motion M-291 by the House of Commons, will the Japanese government realize that their behaviour is not welcome. Japan will regain trust and respect only if they learn from the actions of post-war Germany in true remorse of their wartime atrocities.

THEREFORE, your petitioners call upon the House of Commons to adopt motion M-291.

南京大屠殺 • 七十周年
Nanking Massacre • 70th Anniversary

Remarks of Chairman Lantos on H. Resolution 121

REGARDING COMFORT WOMEN, AT COMMITTEE MARKUP

US HOUSE COMMITTEE ON FOREIGN AFFAIRS, VERBATIM, AS DELIVERED

26 JUNE 2007

I would first like to commend my friend and neighbor in California, our distinguished colleague, Congressman Honda of California, for introducing this important resolution and for all his hard work to give voice to the victims in this matter.

The Government of Japan's unwillingness to offer a formal and unequivocal apology to the women forced to be sexual slaves in World War II stands in stark contrast to its role in the world today. Japan is a proud world leader and a valued U.S. ally, making its unwillingness to honestly account for its past all the more perplexing.

Japan is clearly our greatest friend in Asia and one of our closest partners in the world. The U.S-Japan relationship is the bedrock of peace and stability in the Asia-Pacific region. Our alliance and friendship are based on mutual respect and admiration, and together we have helped promote our shared values of democracy, economic opportunity, and human rights in Asia and throughout the world.

Yet, Japan's refusal to make an official government apology to the women who suffered as so-called "comfort women" is disturbing to all who value this relationship.

The true strength of a nation is tested when it is forced to confront the darkest chapters in its history. Will it have the courage to face up to the truth of its past, or will it hide from those truths in the desperate and foolish hope they will fade with time?

Post-War Germany made the right choice. Japan, on the other hand, has actively promoted historical amnesia.

The facts are plain: there can be no denying that the Japanese Imperial military coerced thousands upon thousands of women, primarily Chinese and Koreans, into sexual slavery during the war.

The continued efforts by some in Japan to distort history and play a game of blame-the-victim are also highly disturbing. Most recently, on June 14th, members of the Japanese government took out an advertisement in the Washington Post that smears the survivors of the comfort women system, including those who testified before our Subcommittee on Asia, Pacific, and Global Affairs.

The advertisement suggests that these women, who were forcibly and repeatedly raped by soldiers, were engaged, and I quote, in "licensed prostitution that was commonplace around the world at the time." This is a ludicrous assertion totally counter to the facts.

Our resolution calls on the Government of Japan to officially acknowledge and apologize for the appalling acts that Imperial Japan committed against the "comfort women." It is a resolution that seeks admission of a horrible truth in order that this horror may never be perpetrated again.

But most importantly, it speaks out for the victims of this monstrous act, who were terrorized and brutalized by men at war. It gives voice to these courageous women whom others have tried to silence through shame, bigotry, and threats of further violence.

It is appropriate that this House stand up for these women, who ask only that the truth be honored.

Finally, let me clear up the intent of Congress: we do not want our good friend and ally Japan to believe we regard them in perpetual punishment for their refusal to acknowledge the comfort women episode.

We want a full reckoning of history to help everyone heal, and then move on.

I strongly support this resolution and I urge all of my colleagues across the aisle to do so likewise. ◆

The advertisement suggests that these women, who were forcibly and repeatedly raped by soldiers, were engaged, and I quote, in "licensed prostitution that was commonplace around the world at the time.

Faleomavaega Condemns Japan's Continued Denial And Refusal To Acknowledge The Attrocities Committed Against Asian And Pacific Island Women During WWII

US HOUSE OF REPRESENTATIVES

27 JUNE 2007

Congressman Faleomavaega announced today that he is very pleased by the overwhelming support of his colleagues in the House Committee on Foreign Affairs during the recent markup of H. Res. 121. H. Res. 121 seeks to express the sense of the House of Representatives that the Government of Japan should formally acknowledge, apologize, and accept historical responsibility in a clear and unequivocal manner for its Imperial Armed Force's coercion of young women into sexual slavery, known to the world as "comfort women", during its colonial and wartime occupation of Asia and the Pacific Islands from 1930s through the duration of World War II.

Initially introduced to the House of the Representatives by former Congressman Lane Evans who championed the cause for years, Congressman Mike Honda re-introduced the resolution in the 110th Congress. H. Res. 121 was subsequently referred to the Subcommittee on Asia, the Pacific, and the Global Environment of which Congressman Faleomavaega is Chairman.

On February 15, 2007, Chairman Faleomavaega conducted a hearing and received testimony from three of the surviving women including Ms. Koon Ja Kim, Ms. Yong Soo Lee, and Mrs. Jan Ruff O'Herne.

On June 26, 2007, the Full Committee on Foreign Affairs reported favorably H. Res. 121 to the House, by a vote of 39 Yeas to 2 Nays. Committee Chairman Tom Lantos has requested Congressman Faleomavaega to manage H. Res. 121 when it is considered on the House Floor for final passage.

The following is a complete copy of Congressman Faleomavaega's statement offered on June 26, 2007 during the Markup of H. Res. 121 by the House Committee on Foreign Affairs.

STATEMENT OF THE HONORABLE ENI F.H. FALEOMAVAEGA BEFORE THE FOREIGN AFFAIRS COMMITTEE MARKUP OF H. RES. 121, JUNE 26, 2006

Mr. Chairman:

First and foremost, I want to thank and commend you and our Senior Ranking Member, Ms. Ros-Lehtinen, for your leadership and efforts and, especially, for your support to bring this proposed legislation in the form of a substitute for markup this morning before our Committee. I also want to thank our colleague, the gentleman from California, Mr. Honda, for his sponsorship of this bill which has the bipartisan support of some 146 Members of the House of Representatives. I also want to make note that this resolution was previously passed by this committee in the last Congress, under the able leadership of our previous Chairman, the gentleman from Illinois, Mr. Henry Hyde. I would be remiss if I did not also mention the name of our former colleague and friend, Mr. Lane Evans also from Illinois, who championed this bill for the past several years.

Mr. Chairman, our Subcommittee on Asia, the Pacific and the Global Environment conducted a hearing in February of this year concerning the proposed bill, and, for the first time ever in the history of the US Congress, three women who were forced into sexual slavery by the Japanese Imperial Army, testified for the record. Ms. Yong Soo Lee and Ms. Koon Ja Kim from Korea, and Ms. Jan Ruff O'Herne now from Australia, were among some 200,000 women from Korea, China, the Philippines, Indonesia and other countries in the Pacific who were forced into prostitution and were severely abused, tortured and even killed by Japanese soldiers before and during the second World War.

Mr. Chairman, there was a lot of discussion during our hearing about the number of apologies made by some of the leaders and prime ministers of Japan, concerning the practice of setting up sexual slave camps during Japanese occupation of several countries throughout Asia before and during World War II. It should be noted, however, that not one Prime Minister has ever made an unequivocal apology on behalf of the Government of Japan, and not even with the support or endorsement of cabinet as a necessary matter of record and operation of a parliamentary system of government.

> *Mr. Chairman, our Subcommittee on Asia, the Pacific and the Global Environment conducted a hearing in February of this year concerning the proposed bill, and, for the first time ever in the history of the US Congress, three women who were forced into sexual slavery by the Japanese Imperial Army, testified for the record.*

As a result of the study which indicates that comfort stations were operated in extensive areas for long periods, it is apparent that there existed a great number of comfort women.

As Mr. Honda eloquently stated in his testimony before our subcommittee, this resolution is simply to call upon "the Government of Japan to formally acknowledge, apologize and accept historical responsibility in a clear and unequivocal manner for its (Japan) Imperial Armed Forces' coercion of young women and girls into sexual slavery during World War II."

In 1993, after a two-year study by the Ministry of Foreign Affairs, under the supervision of the Chief Secretary of Cabinet, an equivalent to the Chief-of-Staff of the White House, Mr. Yahei Kono stated,

The Government of Japan has been conducting a study on the issue of wartime "comfort women" since December 1991. I wish to announce the findings as a result of that study.

As a result of the study which indicates that comfort stations were operated in extensive areas for long periods, it is apparent that there existed a great number of comfort women. Comfort stations were operated in response to the request of the military authorities of the day. The then Japanese military was, directly or indirectly, involved in the establishment and management of the comfort stations and the transfer of comfort women. The recruitment of the comfort women was conducted mainly by private recruiters who acted in response to the request of the military. The Government study has revealed that in many cases they were recruited against their own will, through coaxing coercion, etc., and that, at times, administrative/military personnel directly took part in the recruitments. They lived in misery at comfort stations under a coercive atmosphere.

As to the origin of those comfort women who were transferred to the war areas, excluding those from Japan, those from the Korean Peninsula accounted for a large part. The Korean Peninsula was under Japanese rule in those days, and their recruitment, transfer, control, etc., were conducted generally against their will, through coaxing, coercion, etc.

Undeniably, this was an act, with the involvement of the military authorities of the day, that severely injured the honor and dignity of many women. The Government of Japan would like to take this opportunity once again to extend its sincere apologies and remorse to all those, irrespective of place of origin, who suffered immeasurable pain and incurable physical and psychological wounds as comfort women.

It is incumbent upon us, the Government of Japan, to continue to consider seriously, while listening to the views of learned circles, how best we can express this sentiment.

We shall face squarely the historical facts as described above instead of evading them, and take them to heart as lessons of history. We hereby reiterated our firm determination never to repeat the same mistake by forever engraving such issues in our memories through the study and teaching of history.

As actions have been brought to court in Japan and interests have been shown in this issue outside Japan, the Government of Japan shall continue to pay full attention to this matter, including private researched related thereto.

> *We shall face squarely the historical facts as described above instead of evading them, and take them to heart as lessons of history.*

While substantive, and I commend Mr. Kono for his findings, a Chief Cabinet Secretary of Japan simply does not speak on behalf of the Government of Japan.

In recent months, Prime Minister Abe first denied the existence of such sexual slave camps because of the pressure from the conservative members of his party. Then, he retracted his position because of pressure from leaders of the Asia-Pacific region. Recently, Prime Minister Abe now referred to the issue by stating that he "respects" the finding of the Kono Report of 1993. What does this mean?

Mr. Chairman, I bear no animosity or ill-will towards the people of Japan and I must emphasize that our economic, strategic, and military alliance with Japan could not be better. However, I make this appeal to the leaders of Japan to resolve this issue and move on. There can be no reconciliation without proper acknowledgement. The recognition of this dark chapter of Japan's history of the atrocities and sexual slavery operations authorized and implemented by the Japanese Imperial Army before and during World War II, cannot be denied.

Mr. Chairman, I urge my colleagues to support this resolution. ◆

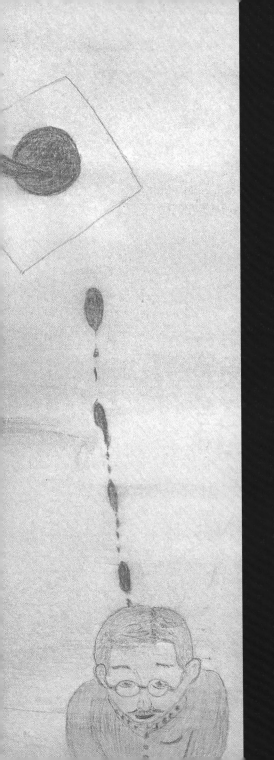

Duk-Kyung Kang
APOLOGIZE BEFORE US, 48.5X37 ACRYLIC ON PAPER, 1995

Awakening

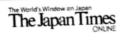

The World's Window on Japan
The Japan Times ONLINE

http://search.japantimes.co.jp/cgi-bin/ed20070802a1.html

EDITORIAL
U.S. House urges clear apology

The U.S. House of Representatives on Monday passed by voice vote a resolution urging Japan to "formally acknowledge, apologize and accept historical responsibility in a clear and unequivocal manner for its Imperial Armed Forces' coercion of young (Asian) women into sexual slavery."

Passage follows approval by the House Foreign Affairs Committee on June 26. The nonbinding resolution says in part that "the United States-Japan alliance is the cornerstone of U.S. security interests in Asia and the Pacific and is fundamental to regional stability and prosperity." But the fact that the full House approved the resolution carries great weight and is a political blow to Prime Minister Shinzo Abe. Similar resolutions on the issue of the Japanese military's use of "comfort women" were submitted four times from 2001 to 2006. This is the first time that the full House has passed such a resolution.

In his April visit to the U.S., Mr. Abe said he sympathizes from the bottom of his heart with former comfort women who went through extreme hardships, and President George W. Bush accepted his apology. Mr. Abe should seriously consider that the

Japanese Prime Minister Shinzo Abe reacts after learning the return of the upper house elections at the Liberal Democratic Party headquarters in Tokyo Sunday, July 29, 2007. Projections indicated the LDP would fall far short of the 64 seats it needs to maintain a majority in the upper chamber, allowing the main opposition Democratic Party of Japan to greatly boost its standing.
(AP Photo/David Guttenfelder)

full House approved the resolution despite Mr. Bush's acceptance of his apology. He should realize that his own attempt in early March to dilute Japan's responsibility for instituting sexual servitude prompted the resolution. At that time, he said testimonies had not proven the existence of coercion in a "narrow sense" — in which "government authorities" intruded into homes and took women away by force.

The resolution in part says that the U.S.-Japan alliance is based on shared vital values such as the preservation and promotion of political and economic freedoms, support for human rights and democratic institutions. But the approval of the resolution shows that many U.S. lawmakers distrust Mr. Abe's attitude toward Japan's human rights violations of the past. Mr. Abe should realize that the problem of perception of history exists not only with Japan's neighbors in Asia but also with the U.S. and could undermine Japan-U.S. ties.

The Japan Times: Tuesday, August 2, 2007

Originally Published
THE JAPAN TIMES, AUGUST 2, 2007

Photo
AP PHOTO/DAVID GUTTENFELDER

Comments from the Canadian Media

CARL FREIRE
THE GLOBE AND MAIL
MARCH 2, 2007

ACTIVISTS, POLITICIANS DENOUNCE JAPANESE PM'S REMARKS ON SEX SLAVES

Prime Minister Shinzo Abe on Thursday said there is no proof the women were forced into prostitution: "The fact is, there is no evidence to prove there was coercion."

His statement contradicted evidence in Japanese documents unearthed in 1992 that historians said showed military authorities had a direct role in working with contractors to forcibly procure women for the brothels, known in Japan as "comfort stations." The remark also cast doubt on a 1993 Japanese government apology to the sex slaves.

Witnesses, victims and even some former Japanese soldiers say many of the women were kidnapped or otherwise forced into sexual slavery at the brothels, where they could be raped by scores of soldiers a day.

THE GAZETTE
MARCH 05, 2007

JAPAN TAKES A STEP BACKWARD

What insulting nonsense. The Japanese are back to denying the 200,000 women taken from Korea and China to serve in Japanese military brothels were not sex slaves at all, but merely "comfort women."

It's a step back — and a big one — from 1993, when Japan admitted the wrongdoing

The truth is inconvenient. But historical accuracy — like admitting 200,000 Korean and Chinese women were enslaved and raped — is still the only path to building a more democratic future.

AL DIONNE
THE OTTAWA CITIZEN
MARCH 07, 2007

JAPAN MUST ADDRESS CRIME OF SEX SLAVES

To say that the 200,000 women (and girls) were not victims but simply business-women who took advantage of a supply-and-demand economy is an insult that defies sane explanation.

Once taken from the woman's family, the best the unfortunate sex slave could hope for was a lifetime scarred by shame and worthlessness, the inevitable result of rape —but even more so in a society based on Confucianism, as is Korea, which places the highest importance on propriety in women. This is the best she could hope for, that is, if she survived the high probabilities of fatal STDs; that is, if she didn't commit suicide to stop the abuse or to abort what would have been a nightmarish pregnancy; that is, if she wasn't executed once she could no longer service Japanese rapists in uniform; that is, if she didn't die from the 20 daily rapes.

To claim that there is no evidence that any of these 200,000 women were coerced is absolutely disgusting.

GLOBE AND MAIL.COM
MARCH 10,2007

FACING UP TO JAPAN'S PAST

But Mr. Abe's brand of patriotism is infused with a troubling revisionist view of history that is reopening old wounds in Asia and making it harder for him to recast Japan's image abroad.

Mr. Abe, whose grandfather was a wartime cabinet minister, is denying that the Japanese military played a direct role in forcing 200,000 Asian women to become sex slaves for Japanese troops between 1937 and 1945. This flies in the face of voluminous historical accounts, reams of testimony from victims and the Japanese government's own previous admission that military authorities had indeed been responsible for the depravities.

Japan's government today is open, democratic and tolerant, while China and several other countries that suffered at the hands of the Japanese are undemocratic

and have a long history of human-rights abuses. But that doesn't relieve Japan of the obligation to recognize publicly its wartime wrongs. Facing up to the past is essential if this ambitious Prime Minister and his government are to move his country forward.

TOM GODFREY
THE TORONTO SUN
MAY 18, 2007

"COMFORT WOMEN" APOLOGY URGED

The sex slavery system was the first and only system for the wholesale raping of young women," Wong said. "The horrendous and inhumane system was devised by the highest commands in Japanese political and military circles.

MARCUS GEE
THE GLOBE AND MAIL
JULY 6, 2007

JAPAN IS STILL PLAYING ATROCITY-DENIAL GAME

Nothing could better illustrate the deep sense of denial that still prevails in Japan over its war record. During a 15-year campaign of aggression in the 1930s and 1940s, Japan conquered much of East and Southeast Asia, subduing its neighbours with a savagery that is still remembered with bitterness.

That savagery included looting, forced labour, massacres of civilians, rape, and the barbaric treatment of prisoners of war. In the case of the so-called comfort women, an estimated 200,000 women from Korea, the Philippines, Indonesia, Burma, China and Taiwan were corralled into brothels for Japanese soldiers.

The A-bomb experience has become a Japanese fetish, blocking out a serious debate about Japan's record of aggression and putting its atrocities in the shade. By far the most important war memorial in Japan is the Hiroshima peace park, a shrine to Japanese suffering. No such memorial exists to commemorate the millions who suffered and died at the hands of Japanese imperialism. It is as if, instead of building a Holocaust memorial in Berlin, Germany put its biggest war monument in Dresden to keep alive the memory of the Allied bombing in February of 1945.

Right-wing Japanese politicians and academics routinely cause outrage in Asia by suggesting that atrocities such as the Rape of Nanking or the comfort-women brothels have been blown out of proportion. It is the Japanese version of Holocaust denial, except that, in Japan, it is not a fringe phenomenon — it is right smack in the mainstream.

Such denials would be unthinkable in Germany, because it has come to terms with its wartime misdeeds and atoned for them. Judged by recent events, Japan has not even begun.

THE TORONTO STAR
AUGUST 12, 2007

OTTAWA MUST END SILENCE

But despite ongoing demands for an official and unequivocal apology and compensation for the surviving women, now in their 70s and 80s, Japan's only response was to issue a carefully worded apology in 1993, never approved by Parliament, after military documents were uncovered showing the army was involved in establishing these brothels.

Even that limited acceptance of responsibility was largely undone earlier this year when Prime Minister Shinzo Abe shamelessly stated there was no proof the comfort women were forced into sexual slavery, prompting an international outcry.

While the NDP and the Liberals support it, the motion needs unanimity and the Conservatives have remained shamefully silent on this issue.

A statement by Parliament would send an important message that Japan needs to make further amends over an episode that still scars generations later and marks a shameful period in its history.

A formal apology from Japan to the surviving comfort women and those who died in despair is long overdue. The Conservative government must join the growing community mounting pressure on this valued ally to do so. ◆

Toronto Star
Pubdate:November 23, 1992　Page: A17　Section:INSIGHT　Edition:AM　Length:1722

An old soldier admits his crime Ichiro Ichikawa ran a brothel of 'comfort girls' for Japanese army

Byline/Source: By Tony Wong TORONTO STAR

Photo Caption: STAR FILE PHOTO: : Japanese soldiers cheer their capture of a Chinese town in 1937. PHOTO: Ichiro Ichikawa

TOKYO - Handing his ticket to an elderly lady at the entrance of the dimly lit barracks, the young soldier walked nervously along the wooden corridor to his first sexual encounter.

Pointing a finger to one of several captive Korean **women**, he chose his unwillingly partner for the night.

The soldier would eventually spend a month's salary on two later visits to the northern China brothel controlled by the Japanese. "I want to experience a woman before I die," he explained when questioned about his extravagance.

At the time, Ichiro Ichikawa found the soldier's remark humorous.

"But today I can understand that the Korean woman probably did not feel the same way he did," he says with quiet understatement.

It's hard to imagine the tiny and bespectacled war veteran as a once-feared official of the Japanese army.

But as a 22-year-old non-commissioned military police officer in Japanese-controlled northern China, Ichikawa had the dubious role of master of the lives of 80 Korean sex slaves, **women** forced into prostitution by the Japanese army.

No soldier could use the brothels without his permission. And the perks of power allowed the former elementary school teacher free reign of the brothels himself.

It's a sordid past that has returned to haunt Ichikawa and the Japanese government over the last year.

The shocking revelations that as many as 1 million Korean, Chinese, Filipina, and Taiwanese **women** were kidnapped and carted off to battlefront brothels is an issue that won't go away in **Japan.**

It has meant a painful re-examination for many Japanese. For others, it has become an issue best swept under an ever-bulging carpet of wartime guilt.

Ichikawa, now 72 and overcome with remorse after decades of silence, has gone public about his tiny but significant role in the lives of the **women**, and is expected to be a star witness in a United Nations inquiry next month.

While several **"comfort women"** have already come forward to press their claims, it has been rare for war veterans such as Ichikawa to speak up.

He talked to The Star in a 4 1/2-hour interview with the aid of an interpreter.

"We did not treat these **women** like human beings. The Japanese government is still saying they weren't forced, but I know they were forced, because I was there," says Ichikawa in his tiny home about an hour's drive north of Tokyo.

Text
TONY WONG

Originally Published
THE TORONTO STAR, NOVEMBER 23, 1992

…A black and white photo of Ichikawa at 22 shows him sitting on his haunches, his legs spread sumo-style, with helmeted head thrown back, a haughty laugh on thin lips.

Said Ichikawa: "We thought we were on top of the world back then."

The Japanese government which initially stonewalled, then denied there were government-sanctioned brothels, now finds itself the target of an increasing number of lawsuits for compensation from "comfort girls" — the way the Japanese to describe sex slaves.

The first lawsuit by a group of comfort women in Korea filed earlier this year still has to be heard. And in China, despite a lack of government support, women are slowly coming forward to make claims for compensation.

As a member of the military police in May, 1943, Ichikawa controlled two army sanctioned brothels in Baicheng. The city, which was in Manchukuo, was brigade headquarters of the Kwang-tung army, a part of the Japanese army which ruled the region.

The larger of the two brothels had about 50 women, all of them Korean.

Korean women were used in China because they did not speak the language and were easier to control, he said.

Some of the women were as young as 17. The eldest was about 30, he said.

"It was sometimes especially hard on the women, because there were never enough," said Ichikawa. "If 500 soldiers came to town and there were only 50 women, then they would each have to take 10 men a piece."

The military police were also responsible for rounding up women from the villages, said Ichikawa.

The M.P.s were feared by everyone, including the soldiers, because they had absolute disciplinary authority, he said.

"The M.P.s would go into an area saying that we were rounding up people for the security of the area, but they were really looking to get girls," said Ichikawa.

"The people would do whatever we said because people who resisted were killed in front of everyone as an example."

Ichikawa said as an M.P. he tortured suspected "spies" by dripping water through the victim's nostrils.

"Their stomachs would swell up after a while and get bloated with the water," he said. "But all you had to do was leave the room and you wouldn't see it, so you wouldn't feel responsible. It was a cruel way of avoiding responsibility."

The veteran insisted throughout the interview that during his two-year reign at the brothels, he did not abuse the women.

"I tried to treat them as best as I could under the circumstances," he said.

Although many of the women caught venereal diseases, medical checks were done once a week and the men were told to use condoms, he said.

The most common problem was urethritis, an inflammation of the urethra, he said.

Daily life was also restricted for the women: They weren't allowed to leave the quarters without permission and they were forbidden to speak or wear Korean clothing, he said.

As far as he knew, none of the women tried to commit suicide during his tenure as they did in other camps, said Ichikawa.

"I can only speak for what I experienced. I don't know how other officers handled the women," he said.

According to one theory, the brothels probably began in the late 1930s after the infamous Rape of Nanjing where thousands of Chinese were massacred.

Wartime documents uncovered by historians called for "comfort quarters" on the theory that satisfying the sexual desires of soldiers would prevent them from committing further rape. In effect, the government set up a system of institutionalized sexual slavery to curb the rapes in the streets that incurred the wrath of the locals.

At the time, commanders were turning a blind eye to rapes by soldiers because they thought it "necessary

to invigorate the soldiers," read one document from a chief of staff of the North China Japanese army in 1938.

The going rate for women at the brothel controlled by Ichikawa was seven yen — almost half the fifteen yen monthly salary of a soldier.

Some brothels would charge a premium for Japanese women, about

Ten yen, while Korean women would cost seven yen and Chinese women, five yen, he said.

Ichikawa himself made 200 yen per month as a non-commissioned officer.

Over the last few months, Japanese newspapers have written scathing editorials spurred on by the horror stories and the wealth of documented evidence uncovered by historians.

"Germany paid compensation to the Jewish victims of Nazism. Both the United States and Canada decided to pay compensation to people of Japanese descent whom they sent to camps during the war. The Japanese government has a responsibility too to pay compensation," said a recent edi-

torial in the popular Mainichi Shimbun newspaper. That editorial was written the day after former Korean comfort woman Sim Mi Ja told reporters at a news conference in Tokyo that she was abducted by soldiers as a 16-year-old school girl.

Sim, now 69, said she embroidered morning glories on the Japanese flag instead of the official cherry blossoms.

An officer at the school told her she had "bad thoughts" and took her into an office where he tried to rape her.

After resisting by biting his ear, Sim was tortured by having a hot iron placed on her shoulder, at which point she fainted.

When she awoke she said she found herself in a room where a soldier came in and demanded sex with her although "I was still suffering from swellings," she said.

"Since then, I served as a lavatory for 20 to 30 soldiers a day, for more than six years," she told reporters.

Ichikawa says he never bothered to ask many of the women how they ended up in the comfort house, because it "wasn't an issue at the time. I really didn't think about it. During the war, lots of terrible things happen."

As his wife pours tea, Ichikawa is noticeably uncomfortable talking about his relationships with comfort women. He admits, though, that he did have "one favorite woman."

"I don't know if she is still alive, but if she is, I will testify on her behalf," he says.

Ichikawa won't reveal the name of the woman. But he is hoping that one day she will see his picture and contact him if she wants to press for compensation.

Ichikawa himself has already paid a high price for his speaking out. He has been ostracized by his fellow Japanese.

"It has been tough because the others (veterans) don't like me talking about the issue," he said.

But the women were the ones who really suffered, during and after the war, said Ichikawa.

The end of the war for them also meant the start of a new life in oblivion, he said.

As the defeated Japanese were fleeing northern China, Ichikawa said he tried to send the women back to their homes because they had already been scorned by their community.

"They were seen as dirty prostitutes, so the local Koreans didn't want to have anything to do with them," he said. "They didn't have a home anymore."

Ichikawa, who spent several years in a Soviet prison for his role in running the brothels, says he's not entirely unselfish in his reasons for going public.

"The Japanese army has already forgotten the veterans who fought in the war and were imprisoned for Japan," he said. "What makes you think they will be in a hurry to help the women?"

A plaque and two silver cups are all he has to show for his time in prison, said Ichikawa.

And that leads to his greatest concern, he says.

"I want the younger people to remember what happened during the war so we don't forget. But the comfort girls are getting old; I'm getting old. I think they're just waiting for us to die so they can forget the past," says Ichikawa with a weary look.

"That is my biggest fear." ◆

Toronto Star				
Pubdate:November 26, 1992	Page: A33	Section:OPINION	Edition:AM	Length:664
Blinkered Japan stumbles through moral landscape				
Byline/Source: By Tony Wong				
Dateline: TOKYO				

TOKYO - As a child, the tales that my mother told me had nothing to do with the Brother's Grimm.

The fairy tales of her youth were interrupted by memories of war, of friends lost, of relatives spirited away.

The Japanese invaded China in 1937, killing up to 10 million over an eight-year period.

But like many children with more imagination than conscience, the stories seemed to me like so much science fiction.

The Japanese once torched her village near the border of Hong Kong, raping and looting as they went, she would say earnestly. They even defecated in some villagers' cooking pots as a sign of contempt.

During those raids, the family would scramble into the hills for refuge.

Once she was separated from my grandparents, spending almost two days with a cousin crouched in a rice paddy while rain poured down on them.

"We would have to stretch out our hands like this," she would gesture cupping her hands, to get water for sustenance. "We didn't think we would live."

As an adult I have a better understanding of the sacrifices my mother was forced to make, of why, many years later, she wanted her family to lack nothing.

There is also a sense of sadness that I wasn't perhaps a little more attentive, a little more supportive.

As a child those stories seemed of a time far away and of little consequence.

Last month, similar memories for many Chinese were dramatically revived as Japanese Emperor Akihito delicately wound his way through China in the first visit of its kind.

Akihito's trip elicited anger from Chinese who were expecting an apology for wrongs inflicted during the invasion.

But from my vantage point in **Japan**, after having spent two months here, that was a little like putting the cart before the horse.

In **Japan**, land of quiet apartheid, it seems there has been no significant change in the status quo since the days of Emperor Hirohito.

Perhaps some wounds may have been salved by an apology but, sadly, those words would be all too shallow given the reality.

Many younger people I talked to, for example, didn't have an opinion on whether the Japanese should apologize to other Asian countries. That's because **Japan**'s aggressive role in the war is largely glossed over in school.

A local newspaper reported statistics that show non-Japanese Asians are treated more harshly than Japanese or even Caucasion foreigners if they are caught breaking the law.

My Japanese-born Korean translator, whose grandparents were

Text
TONY WONG

Originally Published
THE TORONTO STAR, NOVEMBER 26, 1992

One of his worst experiences was when he was forced, like all Koreans, to be finger-printed as an alien, obliged to carry an alien registration card even though he was born here and speaks only Japanese.

…brought to Japan as slaves, told me he's adopted a Japanese name because Koreans, even if they're born in Japan, are still considered foreigners and won't get into the best jobs or schools.

One of his worst experiences was when he was forced, like all Koreans, to be fingerprinted as an alien, obliged to carry an alien registration card even though he was born here and speaks only Japanese.

I listened to this a bit incredulously, until I learned that earlier in the summer, front page headlines were made when the city of Osaka allowed a third-generation Korean resident the proud privilege of applying for employment.

This government-sanctioned discrimination, you realize, is coming from the world's second largest economic power.

It would have been a nice gesture, I suppose, if the emperor had apologized. My mother would have appreciated it, I'm sure.

But that wouldn't change a thing here. Japan, has earned its place as a highly regarded member of the financial world.

But if it is to gain the respect of the international community it must show with some measure of sincerity that it has learned something from recent history.

A Japan that cannot face the past is ill-equipped to face the future. And until things start changing at home, an apology, even from the emperor, would have been a resoundingly hollow gesture. ◆

2007年03月27日　11:29:45　金华新闻网

荷兰女性当年也曾遭日军蹂躏

欧洲媒体赴我市采访

并欲向国际社会揭露日军侵略战争的罪恶

本报讯（记者江胜忠　通讯员何必会）"和你们一样，荷兰的民间人士也向日本政府提出了诉讼和索赔，我们要一起维护正义，揭露罪恶。"昨天，结束了金华细菌战受害情况采访的荷兰国家电视台记者Wouter zwart(中文名：华舒豪)感慨良多。

3月22~23日，Wouter zwart和英国独立制片人Mavk Carey（中文名：马可·卡瑞）和 Mavk Roberts（中文名：马可·罗伯特）等欧洲记者，先后来到我市的侵华日军细菌战义乌展览馆和婺城区汤溪等地，对金华地区细菌战受害者和细菌战诉讼情况进行为期两天的拍摄、采访，并对崇山细菌战遗址和细菌战受害者进行现场采访。3月23日，侵华日军细菌战中国受害诉讼原告团团长王选召集湖南常德、浙江宁波、衢州、江山、丽水、云和、金华各地细菌战受害者诉讼代表约70人，会聚义乌江湾曲江王氏宗祠侵华日军细菌战义乌展览馆，举行细菌战死难者祭奠活动，并就日本最高法院即将对细菌战诉讼案作出三审判决有关事宜进行研讨，欧洲记者进行了全程采访。

Wouter zwart说，荷兰国家电视台和其他欧洲媒体此次深入二战中受害的我市义乌和汤溪等地采访，回欧洲后，他们将推出纪录片向国际社会揭露日军侵略战争的罪恶，维护二战史实。他还介绍，二战期间，日军对荷兰所属西印度群岛的荷兰人以及荷兰战俘犯下罪恶暴行。据历史学家估计，20世纪三四十年代，许多妇女被迫成为日军"慰安妇"，其中也包括不少当时在亚洲居住的荷兰妇女。近年以来，荷兰民间人士曾就日军违反海牙人权协定，而向日本政府提出诉讼和索赔。因此对日索赔者中，除了中国人，还有荷兰人、韩国人、俄罗斯人、英国人。本月16日，荷兰外交大臣马克西姆·费尔哈亨对日本政府当日制定的称未发现有关过去日军曾强征"慰安妇"的直接记述的答辩书提出抗议，并要求日方对此作出解释。

相关文章

新金华市场　　　　　　　　　　　　　　　　　　　　　进入讨论区

金华日报社简介　│关于我们　│网站导航　│联系方式　│广告服务　│新闻报料

Copyright©2003　www.jhnews.com.cn　All Rights Reserved

金华日报社版权所有　浙ICP备05019305号

制作：金华日报社网络部

Opinion Section

http://news.asianweek.com/news/view_article.html?article_id=09b6dc1f9c27d14ee5135c069a116d10

Japan's Shame over Apology

Alan Kenny Wong, Apr 20, 2007

Wu Hsiu-mei, a Taiwanese maid who was handed to Japanese officers by her boss, was forced to have sex with more than 20 Japanese soldiers per day for almost a year. She had multiple abortions and became sterile prematurely. Gil Won-ok, a Korean teenager thrust into sex slavery, caught syphilis and developed tumors in her uterus that were abruptly removed by a Japanese military doctor. "I've felt dead inside since I was 15," said Gil, who, like many other "comfort women," is now unable to bear children.

The world has waited long enough. Now is the time for the Japanese government to formally apologize for their role in coercing women to serve as sex slaves. Between 1937 and 1945, about 200,000 Asian women in conquered countries, mostly Korea, China, the Philippines and Indonesia, were forced by Japan to serve in brothels as so-called "comfort women" for Japan's military. To this day these elderly women have been swept aside, almost forgotten.

Hasty generalizations produced during conflict have gravely hurt Asian Americans, as evidenced by Executive Order 9066, which mandated the Japanese American internment. In that case, what finally brought some ease from the despair that Japanese Americans felt was a formal 1988 apology by President Ronald Reagan. A Japanese apology for sex slavery would similarly relax tensions in Asian America.

The House of Representatives is now considering a nonbinding resolution spearheaded by Japanese American Rep. Mike Honda that would call for Japan to "formally acknowledge, apologize and accept historical responsibility in a clear and unequivocal manner for its Imperial Armed Forces' coercion of young women into sexual slavery." Japanese Prime Minister Shinzo Abe insists that there is, "no historical evidence" of any such matter, and that regardless of the resolution's outcome, Tokyo would not apologize.

Abe's assertion directly contradicts with Japanese documents uncovered in 1992, implicating the military for playing a direct role in procuring women. Moreover, Japanese historians attest that the projected 200,000 victim count is accurate. Even Japanese soldiers, overcome with guilt, have confessed to their shameful acts. Along with live testimony from the victims themselves, how can Abe sleep at night? We cannot continue to allow Japan to erase history.

A simple *mea culpa* would mean the world to these sex slave victims. Java victim Jan Ruff O'Herne told the *New York Times*, "An apology is the most important thing we want — an apology that comes from the government, not only a personal one, because this would give us back our dignity."

The original victims of this dark and hidden tragedy who are speaking out today offer strong, living, compelling proof that the Japanese government must acknowledge and apologize for its egregious criminal acts. This is not a matter of left or right; it is a matter of truth and justice.

Many of the victims have already passed away, and more depart every year. Is it the Japanese government's strategy to wait until they all expire and the world forgets? Let's give back these old women their dignity. By apologizing, Japan would at least dispel decades-old tensions, and start the journey towards forgiveness and reconciliation. Now is the time.

Alan K. Wong is a second-year UC San Diego student and past Congressional Page sponsored by Congresswoman Nancy Pelosi. E-mail him at alankennywong@yahoo.com

Text
ALAN KENNY WONG

Originally Published
ASIANWEEK.COM, APRIL 20, 2007

POINT OF VIEW/ Koken Tsuchiya: Open up stored records on 'comfort women'

http://www.asahi.com/english/Herald-asahi/TKY200704160059.html

04/16/2007

ASAHI SHIMBUN - The government and the Liberal Democratic Party have overreacted to the draft resolution introduced in January to the U.S. House of Representatives that demands Japan formally acknowledge and apologize for forcing women to provide sex for Japanese soldiers during the wars. Similar resolutions have already been adopted by the parliaments of South Korea and Taiwan, so the move is nothing new.

Japan has been strongly urged on repeated occasions to resolve the "comfort women" issue by such international organizations as the United Nations Human Rights Council, the U.N. Committee on Economic, Social and Cultural Rights and the International Labor Organization.

Those facts shows that not only countries that suffered under the Japanese military think Japan has yet to settle the "comfort women" problem, but international organizations that generally maintain neutrality also think so.

Prime Minister Shinzo Abe and Foreign Minister Taro Aso insist "there was no coercion in the narrow sense" and there are "factual errors" in this view of history.

But their arguments do not seem well-grounded. The governments of the Netherlands and South Korea, which both suffered damage from Japan, and these international organizations have conducted their own investigations, including interviews with former comfort women. They have recognized the pain that was inflicted on these women.

On a number of occasions, I have also met and listened to the stories of victims from countries that suffered damage. From what I learned, particularly in countries occupied by Japan such as China and the Philippines, in many cases, women were kidnapped, attacked or confined directly by the military without any involvement by private operators.

Japanese courts have also found evidence of and acknowledged the fact of coercion. The Japan Federation of Bar Associations dispatched members to the related countries to look into damage reports, and it publicized the results. Based on its findings, the federation has four times urged the prime minister to make a formal apology and extend compensation to individuals.

I agree with the theory that the current confusion is caused by the ambiguity of the government's survey released in 1993 and in the wording of the statement issued by then-Chief Cabinet Secretary Yohei Kono.

Meanwhile, there is little evidence that the government has seriously pursued its investigation since 1993. It has been passive at best, not even bothering to interview the surviving comfort women, except for a few in South Korea. Some naysayers have even taken advantage of the

Text
KOKEN TSUCHIYA
Originally Published
IHT/ASAHI, APRIL 16, 2007

…government's inadequate response to this issue to try to discredit the Kono statement.

The government must take the blame for failing to take proper measures. It must look further into the situation and hear from the victims to reveal the true situation of "comfort women" and wartime coercion.

Successive prime ministers have offered "apologies." However neither prime ministers nor foreign ministers have ever personally met with these aging victims.

Listening to these leaders' recent statements in the Diet, I got the impression they have not bothered to read the reports released by the Dutch government after 1993, nor the moving account of "comfort women" on the Indonesian island of Buru that was written more than 30 years ago by prominent Indonesian writer Pramoedya Ananta Toer (1925-2006).

Speculation that is not based on a thorough investigation lacks persuasive power.

It is illogical to argue that just because no official documents can be found that record the coercion, it therefore never happened. While many documents were burned when Japan lost the war, a large number of documents still reside silently in storage rooms at ministries, awaiting a full investigation to reveal the truth.

A proposal to set up a special bureau within the National Diet Library to examine such documents, and bills aimed at settling the "comfort women" problem have been repeatedly submitted to the Diet. Before trying to block the U.S. Congress from adopting its resolution, the Diet should deliberate on these bills.

Some may fear the resolution could cause a rift in Japan-U.S. relations. But denying history is much more detrimental to mutual trust between the two countries.

Mike Honda, the U.S. House of Representatives member who submitted the resolution, insists that only after Japan acknowledges its responsibility can it make peace with its victims and pave the way to stability in the Asia-Pacific region.

The Asian Peace and People's Fund for Women (Asian Women's Fund), which dissolved at the end of March, was regarded by victims and victimized countries as a way for the government to evade responsibility. It is time we reconsider what is in Japan's true national interest. ◆

canada.com
WHERE PERSPECTIVES CONNECT

Wartime rape victims look to Canada for support
Activists urge Ottawa to enact law on declaration demanding reparations

SUE MONTGOMERY
The Gazette

Wednesday, May 16, 2007

Canada should enact into law an international declaration demanding reparations for female victims of wartime sexual violence, so civil court judges here could use it as a tool to rein in abuse within some immigrant communities, a retired Quebec Court judge said yesterday.

Micheline Corbeil-Laramee was among advocates gathered at a Montreal news conference yesterday to promote the Nairobi Declaration, drawn up and signed in March in Kenya by women's activists and survivors of wartime sexual violence.

It aims to lift the shame and secrecy surrounding sexual crimes committed in wartime.

Rape is commonly used as a weapon during conflict to humiliate and dehumanize the "enemy." After hostilities, many women end up destitute as society and family shun them. They can also suffer from AIDS or other sexually transmitted diseases, and receive no psychological support.

Corbeil-Laramee said the Canadian government should endorse the declaration as a way to strengthen the judiciary.

The declaration could also help change the social and cultural behaviour of certain communities, she said.

"If a husband is violent with his wife, it's because it is accepted in his community," she said.

"If a civil suit results, a judge can cite the declaration to say, 'Your way of treating your wife in the country you come from is unacceptable.'

CREDIT: JOHN KENNEY, GAZETTE

From left, Sonia Kambie-Kabbia, of Sierra Leone, Peruvian sociologist Diana Avila Paulette and Lorraine Guay, of the Federation des femmes du Quebec.

CREDIT: JOHN KENNEY, THE GAZETTE

International voices joined yesterday at a Montreal news conference to demand justice and reparations for women who are sexual victims of war.

Text
SUE MONTGOMERY
Originally Published
THE GAZETTE, MAY 16, 2007

Female victims of violence need a place where they feel safe to recount what they lived through so their attackers can be brought to justice.

…"I don't think a judge can say that now."

Yesterday, activists from around the world said female victims of violence need a place where they feel safe to recount what they lived through so their attackers can be brought to justice.

They hope the declaration will improve truth and reconciliation commissions, which have fallen short of providing reparations for women, and guide the International Criminal Court, which has developed a reparations fund.

The declaration was sent to all female MPs. One Liberal, nine Bloc Quebecois members and 12 New Democrats have signed. No one from the Conservative Party has responded.

Stephen Lewis, a former United Nations envoy for HIV/AIDS in Africa, is also a signatory.

Ariane Brunet, co-ordinator of the women's rights program for Montreal-based Rights and Democracy, said the aim is to help women redevelop a sense of self and regain the respect of their community, instead of being seen as victims.

"They want their health back, they want a roof over their head, they want to work and they want justice," said Brunet, who has interviewed several women in countries that have had recent conflicts.

"Those are the four things victims anywhere in the world want." ◊

2007年07月09日　　15:10:40　　　金华新闻网

中日美等国专家在沪研讨细菌战诉讼

7月7日，细菌战诉讼暨细菌战问题国际研讨会在上海教育国际交流中心和上海行政学院会议室举行。当天正值"七七抗战"70周年之际，会议的召开更具有一份特别的纪念意义。

本次会议由侵华日军细菌战中国受害诉讼原告团和细菌战诉讼中国原告日本律师团主办，上海师范大学中国慰安妇问题研究中心协办，美国"世界抗日战争史实维护联合会"暑期教师团受邀作特别报告。湖南常德、浙江义乌（崇山）、金华、衢州、江山、宁波、丽水、云和等地的细菌战受害者代表，加拿大抗日战争史实维护会的代表，香港启志教育基金会代表李诚辉以及浙、苏、沪、鲁等地高校学生的细菌战调查会代表等，共约百人参加了本次研讨会。

上午的会议在上海教育国际交流中心一号会议室举行，由原告团法律顾问刘惠明律师主持，早稻田大学客座讲师张剑波、美国西北大学社会学博士徐彬、东京大学工学博士徐兵担任翻译，日本律师团一濑敬一郎律师作诉讼总结报告，中国律师楼献、国际法学者管建强、宋杰等人作诉讼点评报告，论证了王选为首的细菌战诉讼12年历程的政治、法律、历史等方面的成果、意义和其中存在的一系列问题。从事日军遗留化学武器受害维权的东北律师罗丽娟律师就化学武器受害者诉讼案作了交流报告。从事中国二战劳工美国诉讼中国法律顾问孙靖律师就中国受害劳工在美国法院起诉日本的案件等事宜作了交流报告。浙江衢州原告代表杨大方、侵华日军细菌战义乌展览馆馆长王培根带领各地原告代表向日本律师团赠送锦旗，感谢日本律师团12年来义务为中国受害者维权。

下午的会议在上海行政学院会议室举行，研讨的主题是"细菌战问题的解决与日中友好"。上海行政学院图书馆馆长丁晓强、早稻田大学客座讲师张剑波、细菌战诉讼原告团团长王选、日本京都大学中国近现代史教授江田宪治、日本律师团西村正治律师、日本相模原女子大学吉田义久教授、细菌战诉讼原告团秘书长王培根、衢州细菌战展览馆负责人杨大方、香港启志教育基金会干事长李诚辉、《泣血控诉》作者李晓方、湖南文理学院细菌战罪行研究所朱清如教授、湖南常德对外友协罗建中等人作了会议发言。

世界抗日战争史实维护联合会会长李培德、常务副会长丁元等人作了特邀发言。美国教师团一行17人，由著名爱国侨领、史维会会长李培德带领，6月27日起对中国进行为期两周的学术访问，成员有来自亚洲、北美洲、南美洲、欧洲、非洲各民族的美国教师。如此广泛国际性的教师团自费来华查证日本侵略战争暴行，在国内尚属首次。

（何必会）

Text
江胜忠, 何必会
Originally Published
JHNEWS.COM, JULY 9, 2007

诉讼是为了悲剧不再重演

中·日·美等国专家在沪研讨细菌战诉讼

本报讯（记者江胜忠 通讯员何必会）前天是"七七抗战"七十周年，在上海教育国际交流中心，中、日、美等国专家聚首集会，再次对细菌战诉讼暨细菌战问题进行了研讨。

本次会议由侵华日军细菌战中国受害诉讼原告团和细菌战诉讼中国原告日本律师团主办，上海师范大学中国慰安妇问题研究中心协办，美国"世界抗日战争史实维护联合会"暑期教师团受邀作特别报告。来自金华、义乌、湖南常德、衢州、江山、宁波、丽水、云和等地的细菌战受害者代表、加拿大抗日战争史实维护会的代表、香港昌志教育基金会代表李诚辉以及浙、苏、沪、鲁等地高校学生的细菌战调查会代表等，共约百人参加了本次研讨会。

研讨会由原告团法律顾问刘惠明律师主持，日本早稻田大学客座讲师张剑波·美国西北大学社会学博士徐彬、东京大学工学博士徐兵担任翻译，日本律师团一濑敬一郎律师作诉讼总结报告，中国律师楼献、国际法学者管建强、宋杰等人作诉讼点评报告。论证了王选为首的细菌战诉讼12年历程的政治、法律、历史等等方面的成果、意义和其中存在的一系列问题。从事日军遗留化学武器受害维权的东北律师罗丽娟律师就化学武器受害者诉讼案作了交流报告。从事中国二战劳工美国诉讼中国法律顾问孙靖律师就中国受害劳工在美国法院起诉日本的案件等事宜作了交流报告。衢州原告代表杨大方、侵华日军细菌战义乌展览馆馆长王培根带领各地原告代表向日本律师团赠送锦旗，感谢日本律师团十二年如一日义务为中国受害者维权。

世界抗日战争史实维护联合会会长李培德·常务副会长丁元等人作了特邀发言。李培德认为，研讨的主题"细菌战问题的解决与日中友好"非常切合当今形势，诉讼或维权的目的是为了悲剧不再重演，也为了中日世代友好下去。

'Comfort woman' shares her painful past

GEOFFREY YORK
FROM MONDAY'S GLOBE AND MAIL
JULY 9, 2007 AT 7:20 AM EDT

SHANGHAI
— At the age of 81, stooped and frail, Lin Yanjin is one of the last remaining witnesses to the truth about Japan's wartime sex slaves.

For five months in 1943, she was raped every day by Japanese soldiers who occupied the Chinese island of Hainan. She remembers the beatings and cigarette burns that left her swollen and in constant pain. She was 17 years old.

Yet the details of her story - and many similar accounts - are increasingly denied and dismissed by political leaders in Japan, where nationalism and patriotism are a rising force.

Even the Prime Minister, Shinzo Abe, recently claimed that the "comfort women" were not coerced.

Visitors look at portraits of women forced to become comfort women by the Japanese military during the Second World War at the historical museum of sexual slavery in Gwangju, South Korea. *(Han Jae-ho/Reuters)*

Last month, 44 Japanese members of Parliament bought a full-page advertisement in The Washington Post to allege that the comfort women of the 1940s were licensed prostitutes who were often better paid than Japanese military officers.

For the survivors of the system of sexual slavery at Japanese military bases, the latest denials have added a deep insult to a horrific injury.

"I was very angry when I heard such news," Ms. Lin said. "The Japanese government is still denying it. But it really happened. It happened to me in Hainan. And I'm still suffering from the violence they did to me."

An estimated 200,000 women - mostly Chinese and Korean - were forced into sexual servitude under Japanese wartime occupation. Of the Chinese victims, only 47 are still alive and willing to speak out. Every year, more of the survivors are dying.

The death of 83-year-old Yuan Zhulin in early 2006 meant the loss of another witness. In 1941, when she was a 21-year-old woman in a Japanese-occupied region of southern China, she was recruited by Japanese soldiers who told her that she would work as a hotel cleaner.

Instead, she was transferred to a "comfort station" at a Japanese military base. She tried to resist, but soldiers forced her into the station with bayonets and she was beaten by the Japanese owner of the station.

Ms. Yuan had a two-year-old baby at the time, but she was forcibly separated from the child, who starved to death as a result. After the war, her injuries left her unable to have any more children.

"My mother was definitely coerced to be a comfort woman," said her adopted daughter, 60-year-old Chen Fei.

Text
GEOFFREY YORK

Originally Published
THE GLOBE AND MAIL, JULY 9, 2007

…"To the last possible moment, she fought against the Japanese military."

Her mother believed that China and Japan should learn from their history, Ms. Chen said. "The Japanese government is refusing to admit what it did," she said. "It refuses to show any repentance. This is a violation of historical facts. I'm very angry and frustrated by it."

Ms. Chen and Ms. Lin spoke to a group of Canadian high-school students in Shanghai on Saturday. It was the 70th anniversary of the beginning of Japan's full-scale invasion of China's biggest cities in 1937.

The women spoke at Shanghai Normal University, where China has opened its first official archives on the ordeal of the "comfort women," as the sex slaves were euphemistically known in Japan.

The archives, which opened last week, includes a Japanese soldier's condom and other evidence gathered from the remains of the comfort stations in China.

Its director, history professor Su Zhiliang, says the Japanese military created about 160 comfort stations in Shanghai alone. Using old photographs and documents, he has tracked down the exact addresses of many of them. Some of the Chinese comfort women were girls as young as 12 years old, he said. The girls and women were forced to provide sex to as many as 50 soldiers a day.

Ms. Lin was a peasant woman, working in a rice paddy, when she was abducted by Japanese soldiers and taken to a military base in 1943.

"We were treated worse than pigs and dogs," she said. "We were not given clothes. We were violated in the daytime and the nighttime."

As she told her story to the Canadian students, Ms. Lin spoke in a weak and trembling voice. At first she was expressionless, but later she wept repeatedly. Many of the students cried, too, as they listened.

"When they raped me, I resisted strongly, but they were too strong," she said. "They beat me and burned my face with cigarettes. My whole face and body was swollen. I wanted to run away, but there was no way to escape. I cried all day."

After she had survived five months in captivity, her parents managed to bribe some Chinese security men, giving them chickens in exchange for their help in obtaining their daughter's release from the military base.

Even two months after her release, she was still seriously ill, with blood in her urine. But her ordeal was not over. Japanese soldiers often came to her village, and some of them raped her again.

After the war, it was many years before she was able to marry. "I felt very ugly, because of the violence against me," she said. "I felt that I could not think of love."

When she eventually married, she became pregnant but miscarried and was never able to have a child, though she adopted a son. "My womb was never able to recover from the trauma of what was done to me," she said. "I still feel the pain today, physically and emotionally. My whole life was destroyed by what I suffered. I still feel very bad. I feel that no man can ever like me." For most of her life, Ms. Lin has lived in poverty in a shabby hut in the hills of Hainan. In recent years she has received a small income supplement from the researchers at Shanghai Normal University.

Her family members did not want her to travel to Shanghai to describe her wartime suffering. The ordeal of the comfort women is still a taboo subject in Hainan's villages — a source of shame for the villagers. It took courage for her to speak out, her supporters say.

"I just want to have peace of mind," Ms. Lin said. "I insist that the Japanese government should apologize and pay compensation, so that I can console my mind."

The students, from schools near Vancouver, were moved by her words. "It's very important that everyone should know about this, because otherwise history could be repeated," said Sara Carlyle, a Grade 12 student at North Delta Secondary School in Delta, B.C.

She told Ms. Lin: "You are our inspiration. These things will not go in vain. They will be known, and they will make a difference."

Megan Lum, a Grade 10 student at Fleetwood Park Secondary School in Surrey, B.C., said it was "heartbreaking" to hear Ms. Lin's story.

"What happened was horrible," she said. "It's even more horrible that we don't know about it and it's not taught in school." ◆

> *"I just want to have peace of mind," Ms. Lin said. "I insist that the Japanese government should apologize and pay compensation, so that I can console my mind."*

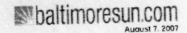

Home > News > Sun Editorials

Gentlemen of Japan

August 1, 2007

Japanese voters repudiated Prime Minister Shinzo Abe on Sunday - and in no uncertain terms - over economic mismanagement. But if it slows down his desire to remilitarize Japan, that can only be a good consequence.

The ruling Liberal Democratic Party lost control of the upper house of parliament, and the opposition Democratic Party of Japan is foursquare against Mr. Abe's nationalist tendencies.

An immediate result may be the withdrawal of Japanese ships from the Indian Ocean once their authorization expires in November. They are there ostensibly to help combat terrorism, but critics see them as token gestures of support for the U.S. war in Iraq.

Mr. Abe and his allies - including many in the Bush administration - believe that 60 years after the end of World War II, it is time for Japan to take on the normal burdens of defense, much as Germany has. And they would be right, except for one important condition: Unlike Germany, Japan has refused to come to terms with its wartime history. That must come first.

On Monday, the U.S. House of Representatives called on Japan to apologize for its treatment of an estimated 200,000 "comfort women," or sex slaves, during the war. As skeptical as we are of congressional resolutions regarding other countries' histories, it was interesting to see the Japanese government immediately express its regret - over the resolution, not over the use of comfort women.

In fact, over the years, various Japanese leaders have offered pro forma apologies to those abused by imperial forces, but they were marked by their evident insincerity. Mr. Abe himself apologized, grumpily, to the comfort women last spring - and then immediately went on to say he doubted that they had been coerced into the army's brothels.

To some Americans, this may all seem somewhat academic and beside the point - but in the Philippines and China and Korea, the refusal of Japan to own up to its war crimes is still a very real issue.

An unrepentant and remilitarized Japan would create nothing but bad feelings and trouble in East Asia. Of course Japan should one day conduct itself as a normal country would. The place to begin is in coming to terms with its history - as a normal country would.

Classified
  Place an ad
  Jobs
  Cars
  Homes
  Apartments
  Personals
  Pets
  Grocery Coupons

Maryland Weather

Traffic

News

Sports

Lifestyle

Business

Opinion
  Editorials
  Letters to the Editor
  Op/Ed
  Talk Forums
  Columnists

Travel

Shopping

Resources
  Print Edition
  Wireless Edition
  RSS Feeds
  Newsletters/Alerts
  Archives

Services
  Subscriber Services
  Get home delivery
  Media Kit
  Reader Rewards
  Sun Store
  Contests
  Events
  Special Sections
  Fifty Plus
  Place an ad
  Speakers' Bureau
  FAQs
  Contact Us

Originally Published
BALTIMORESUN.COM, AUGUST 1, 2007

worldjournal.com
世界新聞網

http://www.worldjournal.com/wj-sf-news.php?nt_seq_id=1561927

舊金山新聞

親訪慰安婦 灣區教師震撼

林亞金老婦人憶述60年前悲歌 史維會全美教師培訓團成員陪著落淚

【本報記者黃美惠庫比蒂諾報導】安德烈‧喬登（Andre Jordan）一直夢想能到中國去，看看長城有多雄偉。13日他從中國回來了，最想說的卻不是長城，而是在上海見到的一位老婦人，一位海南島出身的「慰安婦」林亞金。

喬登、華裔的楊欣（Anne Yang）都是世界史維會2007年全美教師培訓團赴中國考察的成員。11位成員以及世界史維會長李培德、常務副會長丁元以及英國浩劫中心的代表等，剛完成在中國上海等地的訪問回到灣區。

喬登老師(左)和華裔的楊欣都說，在中國直接和慰安婦談話，是今生難得的經驗。
（記者黃美惠攝）

喬登執教於亞裔生占六成多的亞伯拉罕‧林肯高中，他表示，有關中國二戰時所遭受的浩劫，他發現在網站上的內容根本不敷教學上的需要。此次中國之行，收穫豐盛，都成為將來授課時的材料。喬登說，現在的孩子抱怨著很多身旁的小事，「可是聽聽這位林大娘的遭遇吧！」

林亞金是海南島的黎族人，1943年和友人在家附近的稻田被日本兵強押走時才十多歲，她逃，卻因為跌倒而被追，瘦小的她掙不脫，終被兩名日軍強暴，接著是日復一日被輪暴的日子，沒有錢，也沒有食物，日本人放她每天回家，再每天去報到，她不敢不從，因為日本人說她如果不來就殺她全家。

「林亞金生病了，父母還怪她生病吃藥花家裡的錢，」喬登一邊讀自己記下的日記一邊說，他記得林亞金就是講到這裡時，眼淚開始掉下來。社會和家庭的不諒解，比起她花三個月治療性病後又被迫回到慰安所工作，並且被送到各地去當慰安婦，更讓她傷心。

她因為不能生育領養了一個兒子，兒子和兒媳至今仍嫌棄她、鄙視她。喬登說，林亞金今

Text
黃美惠
Originally Published
WORLD JOURNAL, JULY 14, 2007

年82歲，講到當年兩個朋友的命運
還會哭，有一位因為要逃跑，被日
本人當著全村的面前砍頭，另一位
懷孕了，日本人用刀切開她的子
宮，「可憐她小小的子宮，只有水
瓶大小。」

喬登說，林亞金向大家訴說自己的
故事，這個六十多年前的每個細節
都記得一清二楚，當年她沒法睡，
噩夢連連，到今天都是孤獨的。
「我將永遠記得她的眼神，」喬登
說，他在上海見到林大娘兩次，中
間隔了約一星期，第二次是在旅店
走廊，她看到他，記起這個美國來
的黑人聽過她的故事，「她對我笑
了一笑，」喬登說，他希望這位目
前生活仍窮苦的老婦人有生之年，
還能有一點歡笑的可能。

楊欣在灣區從事企業顧問的工作，
她也強調，美國的初中、高中教
材，二戰日本在亞洲的暴行部分幾
乎空白，她在中國所見所聞，回來
後都告訴周遭的人。

丁元說，此行新華社記者、中央電
視台都報導，一行人連在紫禁城都
有遊客認出他們是灣區去的。丁元

喬登老師(左)和華裔的楊欣都說，在中國直接和慰安婦談話，是今乍難
得的經驗。

(記者黃美惠攝)

說，聽慰安婦現身說法令人鼻酸，「林亞金敘述的那位子宮被日本兵剖開的朋友，接下來
的事更悲慘，因為日本兵把這名十多歲懷孕少女的子宮拉出來，掛在樹上當槍靶掃射。」
丁元說，日本政府怎麼能不為慰安婦正式道歉？

2007-07-14

Chung: `Comfort women' find ally in Honda

By L.A. Chung
Mercury News Columnist

To some, it may seem odd that U.S. Rep. Mike Honda of Campbell is pressing for a House resolution urging Japan to apologize for its World War II enslavement of "comfort women," 60-plus years ago, even if, as he says, it's "the right thing to do."

House Resolution 121, which condemns the Japanese military's forcing up to 200,000 women throughout the Pacific Theater into sexual slavery for soldiers in the 1930s and through World War II, appears headed for a full vote of the House before the August recess.

It's a non-binding resolution that packs a punch, as evidenced by the members of the Asia Pacific news media who packed the chambers where the House Foreign Affairs Committee passed it on an overwhelming 39-2 vote last month. Japan, since World War II, has been a steadfast U.S. ally, and this week warned that the resolution would seriously damage relations.

Yet there it is, the resolution that has House Speaker and San Francisco Democrat Nancy Pelosi's backing, being carried by a third-generation Japanese-American, that says the House of Representatives believes Japan must "formally acknowledge, apologize and accept historical responsibility in a clear and unequivocal manner" for its Imperial Armed Forces' coercion of young women into sexual slavery.

Watched closely

"This is not Japan-bashing," he said, echoing statements he has made since he pressed through a similar resolution for wartime atrocities, in the state Assembly in 1999. "I'm proud to be of Japanese-American descent. But it's about being willing to make amends."

The comfort-women story is a horrific page from the saga of many atrocities that the Imperial Army committed as it cut a swath through China, Taiwan, Indonesia, the Philippines and the Pacific Islands.

The euphemism both conveys the official practice and masks the horror of being forced to service Japanese soldiers craving release from mind-numbing days of waging war.

Text
L.A. CHUNG
Originally Published
MERCURYNEWS.COM, JULY 18, 2007

In February, three elderly women - two Korean, one Dutch taken by the Japanese from Indonesia - testified to the committee of their experiences of being kidnapped and raped systematically. They spoke of years of shame, bitterness and the hollow feeling that is akin to living as though one had already died, almost like a ghost.

"Those who were kidnapped, coerced and taken away to be used as sex slaves - sometimes mutilated and killed - had their youth and dignity taken away from them," Honda said when I asked him why.

Reparations are often mentioned. But it is really about the heart, he said. About reconciliation.

Honda's determination to carry such a resolution is directly related to his experience as a young person seeking reconciliation through redress for the World War II internment of Japanese-Americans, Honda said. That act of Congress brought about healing, he said.

How sorry?

In Japan, individual high-ranking officials have apologized over the years. But the Diet, Japan's parliament, has resisted passing a formal apology. A fund to help compensate comfort women was rejected by many because the Japanese government played no role.

Apologies have been followed by high-level visits to the Yasukuni Shrine, where 14 convicted war criminals are buried. Textbooks undergo a whitewashing. Prime Minister Shinzo Abe said in March that there was "no evidence" to prove comfort women were coerced. No wonder apologies seem insincere.

Sure, Honda admits, America has its own amends to make, and should.

"Reconciliation doesn't have a timeline," he says. Except one. I'd hope these octogenarians live to see an apology.

Virginia Hsiao, 14
WHO IS RESPONSIBLE FOR THIS BLOODSHED? WHAT WAS THE ROLE AND WHERE
WAS THE JAPANESE EMPEROR DURING THE SECOND WORLD WAR? THOUSANDS OF
INNOCENT PEOPLE WERE KILLED. THOSE WHO SURVIVED THE JAPANESE ARMY'S
COLD-BLOODED ACTS ARE STILL HAUNTED BY THEIR HORRIBLE NIGHTMARE.

Thank You

TORONTO ALPHA AND HARMONY MOVEMENT

GRATEFULLY ACKNOWLEDGE THE GENEROUS CONTRIBUTION FROM

The Avery-Tsui Foundation

IN THE PRODUCTION OF

"Iris Chang — The Rape of Nanking"

FILM SPONSOR

IDA AND GLENN CHAN

FILM SPONSOR

ADA TANG

FILM SPONSOR

WENDY AND ALAN LI

FILM SPONSOR

LENA AU-YEUNG

FILM SPONSOR

CBC DRAGON INC.

FILM SPONSOR

ELLEN PUN

EDUCATION SPONSORS

EDUCATION SPONSORS

IDA AND GLENN CHAN

LENA AU-YEUNG

EDUCATION SPONSORS

中華食品公司

EDUCATION SPONSORS

ADA TANG   MARY NG

PEACE SPONSORS

瑪莉諾學校
Marilake
Heritage School
416.292.1515

WINNIE & ROY

TICKET SPONSOR
WEBSITE SPONSOR

PE PharmEng®
International Inc.

南京大屠殺・七十周年
Nanking Massacre • 70th Anniversary

STUDY TOUR SPONSORS

**CHRISTINE AND
JOSEPH Y.K. WONG**

FIONA & DEREK CHAN

CURRICULUM SPONSORS

STUDY TOUR SPONSORS

DANNY ZHANG

ASTER AND TAK NG LAI

**CANAAN CHINESE
INTERNATIONAL
BUFFET
RESTAURANT**

WU'S TEXTILE INC.

**IRENE AND
FRANK CHAU**

**CONGEE QUEEN
皇后名粥**

南京大屠殺・七十周年
Nanking Massacre • 70th Anniversary

AT FINANCIAL	**ALPHA PANG**	**CONNIUM MANAGEMENT INC.**
ALEX YUAN	**ANDY IP**	**EDWARD LIN MEDICINE**

PROFESSIONAL CORPORATION	**PATCHES AND LABELS CO**	**HENRY HO**
FRANCIS HUI	**HELENA AND TERRY O'CONNOR**	**AT FINANCIAL**

COMMUNITY SPONSORS A

DR. JIMMY POON

DR. JOSEPH K. WONG

KAI WING TSANG, BARRISTERS,

SOLICITORS & NOTARIES

MONCO PRODUCE INC.

DR. AND MRS. PARE

COMMUNITY SPONSORS A

SAM K.S. CHIU

SARA AND DANIEL MOK

SARAH YIN PING LEUNG

SHIRLEY AND ROBERT TANG

STEPHEN YAU

T.C. CHAN

COMMUNITY SPONSORS A

TAUNEY YU

MR. YIP

陳繼怡

頤康耆英會

火車頭

檸檬草

MR. & MRS. WILLIAM & ANITA KWONG

騰龍閣

XE LUA VIETNAMESE CUISINE

CANCO DIEP

MR. G.T. LAU

DR. ALEX CHAN

MARIETTA NUYENS AND CHEUK KWAN

MR. WILL SUNG

MRS. H.C. LEE

MR. & MRS. KAI KI LUI

KENNY WAN CHARTERED ACCOUNTANT

KINGS AUTO

MS. LUCIA LEE

LUNG KUNG TIN YEE ASSOCIATION

MS. MARIA YAU

ONTARIO SOCIETY FOR CHINESE EDUCATION

COMMUNITY SPONSORS B

PAUL KWONG	SUSANA NG	STANLEY KWAN	THE PHARMASOURCE INC.
THRIFTY CAR RENTAL	雅樂居	WINNIE NG AND EUGENE YAO	Y.C. KWOK

COMMUNITY SPONSORS B

	頤康胡陳金枝松柏新村	上海新天地	新世界皇宮酒樓
		PEARL HARBOURFRONT CHINESE CUISINE	強記雞粥

COMMUNITY SPONSORS C

LANDPOWER REAL ESTATE LTD.	LEMONGRASS	AMY TSE	ERNEST NG
RON K.T. SO	RONNY TSANG	SU MENG WANG	VENNE AND DENNIS LAM

南京大屠殺・七十周年
Nanking Massacre • 70th Anniversary

COMMUNITY SPONSORS C

	WINNIE & ALEX LAU	WONG KUNG HAR WUN SUN ASSOCIATION	陳容超巾

COMMUNITY SUPPORTERS

ACCE	AMY AND CLIFFORD PAK	MS. ANGELA MA	ANNE PICK AND BILL SPAHIC
CANGO CONSULTING GROUP	CHOY FOONG INT'L TRADING CO. INC.	CONNIE SAM	DAVID CHAN
DAVID CHUNG	DEREK NG	DONALD Y. CHEN	ELEANOR AND ERIC WONG

COMMUNITY SUPPORTERS

ELIZABETH AND DIGBY COOK	EMPIRE ORIENTAL CUISINE	FORESTVIEW CHINESE RESTAURANT	GO TO EAT INC.
GLORIA FUNG	HELEN LU	MR. HENRY LEE	HILDA AND ALBERT WONG
HUNG HING CHEUNG	JAMES LI	JOANNE CAMPBELL AND GORDON CRESSY	JOE CHAN

COMMUNITY SUPPORTERS

JOSEPHINE AND JIM CHAN	KOON TO TAM	KIU FAI CHAN	LARRY AU
NORMAN BEACH	NGOC ANN JEWELLERY CO.	PATRICK C.R. NG	PAULINE TONG
PEARL HARBOURFRONT CHINESE CUISINE	PETER KWAN	PUI-KING LEUNG	RAYMOND LEUNG

COMMUNITY SUPPORTERS

ROSALINE SUNG	PRO SCHOLAR INC.	R SHOP	MR. & MRS. SAMUEL & HELEN CHAN
SALLIE TAI	SIMPSON CHAN	SUPREMO VINO INC.	TAMMY AND STEPHEN MOK
WING LEUNG LAM	馮金枝	郭麗嫦	馬珍波

COMMUNITY SUPPORTERS

| | TERENCE WONG | RICE PAPER | SYNERGETIC MARKETING AND PROMOTION INC. |
| | PHILIP WAH | CANADIAN SOCIETY OF CHINESE MEDICINE AND ACUPUNCTURE | TERENCE WONG |

Toronto ALPHA Board of Directors

B.C. ALPHA Board of Directors

* Education/Projects sponsored by Harmony Education Foundation

The Nanking Massacre— 70 Years of Amnesia

2007 Events Committee

EDITORIAL COMMITTEE
Flora Chong
Prof. Albert Ng
Dr. Joseph Y.K. Wong, C.M.
Linna Xu

ART DIRECTOR
Prof. Albert Ng

GRAPHIC DESIGNERS
Linna Xu
Albert Ng

GRAPHIC DESIGN ASSISTANT
Jane Wang

PROOFREADING
Flora Chong
Stanley Loo
Dr. Joseph Y.K. Wong, C.M.

PRODUCTION
Eric Tam, Bygraphics

PREPRESS
Plate Ready Inc.

CHAIR
Dr. Joseph Y.K. Wong, C.M.

TREASURERS
Peter Li
Susana Ng
Josephine Yuen

COORDINATOR
Flora Chong

MEMBERS
Leanne Kuk
Betty Lam
Gordon Lam
Irene Lam
Ivy Lam
Adam Poon
Joseph Tsang
May Wong
Nancy Yan

FUNDRAISING DINNER CO-CHAIRS
Alan Kwong
Hugo Lam

PREMIERE CO-CHAIRS
Dennis Lam
Jeffrey Lam

CONCERT CO-CHAIRS
Aster Lai
Helen Lu, O. ONT
Oi-Yuk Lo
Rosaline Sung

DINNER DECOR AND CENTRE PIECES
Sam Chiu
Sarah Leung
Helena O'Connor
Terry O'Connor
Christine S. W. Wong

CONCERT MUSIC DIRECTOR & CONDUCTOR
Tak-Ng Lai

CONCERT PRODUCTION MANAGER
Ricky Chan

AUDIO/VISUAL CONSULTANT
Duncan Au

IT/WEB SUPPORT
Anita Chiu
Simon Chow
Stanley Loo

PHOTOGRAPHER & VIDEOGRAPHER
Perry Chan
Bang Ho
Mandy Ou

PUBLICATIONS
Kevin Wong

Volunteers

Adam Poon
Alan Kwong
Alice Wong
Albert Ng
Alex Siu
Alex Tsui
Allan Wu
Amy Chan
Andrea Chun
Andy Hon
Andy Lam
Angela Wan
Anita Chiu
Anna Kan
Annie Lam
Anson Poon
Aster Lai
Bang Ho
Barion Mo

Bernard Ng
Betty Lam
Betty Tang
Bonita Ng
Bonnie Shea
Cathy Chan
Cecilia Shea
Cherie Tsang
Christine S.W. Wong
Colin MacNeil
Colin Yu
Connie Lau
Conrad Chan
Cristina Senjug
Darwin Chan
David Wong
Deborah Maak
Deepa Karamjeet
Dennis Lam

Dora Tam
Duncan Au
Eleanor Wong
Eric Lam
Erika Chong
Eugene Koh
Eugene Man
Flora Chong
Francis Lee
Fred Lee
Frederick Lam
Fu Zhou Chen
Gary Ng
Gencan Lam
Genuine Lam
George Hall
George Lau
Gladys Yuen
Gloria Fung

Gloria Chan
Gloria Lam
Gordon Lam
Hai Bin Zhang
Han Li
Helen Lu
Helena O'Connor
Honford Chong
Hugo Lam
Irene Lam
Ida Tsang
Ivy Lam
Jaclyn Ma
James Chung
Jane Campbell
Jane Wang
Janette Kwan
Jeffrey Lam
Jeffrey M.H. Lam

Jennifer Au
Jennifer Wan
Jenny Lau
Jerry Lau
Jia Ming Wang
Jihyun Choi
Johnny Chung
Joseph Tsang
Joseph Y.K. Wong
Joseph Wan
Josephine Yuen
Judy Yeung
Kelvin Ng
Kenneth Ng
Kevin Wong
Kimberly Cheah
Laura Jones
Leanne Kuk
Linna Xu

Lorraine Lee
Mandy Ou
Maria Yau
Maria Szeto
Mary Zee
Matthew Ho
May Wong
Meng Wang
Michael Yuen
Michael Wong
Michelle Meng
Ming-Jarm Lau
Nancy Yan
Nelson Chak
Nicholas Lam
Oi-Yuk Lo
Patricia O'Reilly
Perry Chan
Peter Li

Peter Liu
Rainbow Mui
Randall Yu
Rebecca Chu
Ricky Chan
Robert Lato
Rosa Ng
Rosaline Sung
Sai Kit
Sam Chiu
Sarah Giddens
Sarah Leung
Senam Lam
Sherman Lam
Simon Chow
Stanley Loo
Stephanie Chau
Stephen Fu
Suki Fu

Susana Ng
Tak-Ng Lai
Terry O'Connor
Tian Yue
Tommy Hui
Tony Yu
Violet Lam
Vivienne Wong
Ying Lau
Yonnie Chung
Yvonne Chan